What Works in Policing?

Operations and Administration Examined

|||| |||||||||||| ||| |||||||||||||||||||||||||||||||| P9-CKP-382

Edited by

Gary W. Cordner
Eastern Kentucky University

Donna C. Hale
Shippensburg University

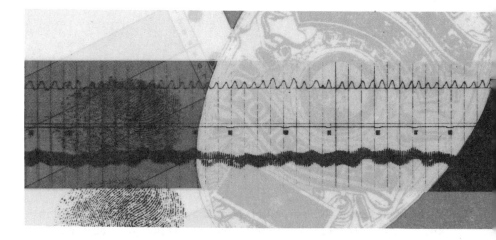

Academy of Criminal Justice Sciences
Northern Kentucky University
402 Nunn Hall
Highland Heights, KY 41076

Anderson Publishing Co.
Criminal Justice Division
P.O. Box 1576
Cincinnati, OH 45201-1576

Riverside Community College
Library
4800 Magnolia Avenue
Riverside, California 92506

HV 8141 .W43 1992

What works in policing?

What Works in Policing?
Operations and Administration Examined

Copyright © 1992 by Anderson Publishing Co. and
                    Academy of Criminal Justice Sciences

All rights reserved. No part of this book may be used or reproduced in any manner without written permission from Anderson Publishing Co. and the Academy of Criminal Justice Sciences.

ISBN 0-87084-015-0

Library of Congress Catalog Number 91-70612

Kelly Humble *Managing Editor*   *Project Editor* Gail Eccleston

Cover Design by John H. Walker

Acknowledgments

First and foremost, we wish to thank the contributors for their hard work, patience, and understanding over the last three years. Working with them has been a very rewarding experience for both of us.

We gratefully acknowledge Evelyn Mynes, who assisted with manuscript processing at Eastern Kentucky University, and Michael Mason of Shippensburg University, who assisted in compiling the author and subject indices.

Gary extends special thanks to Suzanne Armetta for her support and willingness to endure the demands created by projects like this one. Donna's special thanks go to Tom Austin, who listened, advised, and agreed to reschedule vacations to accommodate her research, writing, and publication deadlines.

We both thank Anna Victoria Wilson, Larry Gaines, Robert Bohm, Richard Lumb, and Vince Webb for their roles in bringing this volume into the ACJS Monograph Series.

—Gary W. Cordner
Donna C. Hale

Contents

Introduction

This book presents the latest evidence and a variety of viewpoints on the effectiveness of some of the most important elements of police operations and police administration. Each chapter focuses on one aspect of the police business and asks several questions:

- What is current practice?
- What works?
- What do we know?
- What don't we know?

Taken together, these chapters go a long way toward summarizing what we know about *What Works in Policing*. However, it is quite important to recognize that the question, "What works?" is much more complex and much deeper than it may seem at first glance. Ultimately, it is a question that goes to the core of a number of issues related to the role of the police in a free society. We point out some of these issues below to prevent anyone from incorrectly thinking that the determination of efficient and effective methods of policing can be a simple and straightforward exercise.

MULTIPLE OBJECTIVES

If policing had a single overarching objective, as businesses have with "maximizing profit" or "maximizing profit share," determining what works would be much easier. For example, if "maximizing citizen satisfaction with police services" was the single objective of a police department, then, through research and trial and error, those techniques that contributed most to citizen satisfaction could be discovered and implemented. It would take effort and ingenuity to discover such methods, and refinements would certainly have to be made over time as circumstances and peoples' preferences changed, but efficiency and effectiveness could reasonably be assured.

Of course, the police actually have multiple objectives. References to the twin objectives "protect and serve" are not uncommon; another well-known pair is "law enforcement" and "order maintenance;" a popular triad is "protect life, protect property, and maintain order." A more detailed listing has been identified by Goldstein (1977:35):

1. To prevent and control conduct widely recognized as threatening to life and property (serious crime).

2. To aid individuals who are in danger of physical harm, such as the victim of a criminal attack.

3. To protect constitutional guarantees, such as the right of free speech and assembly.

4. To facilitate the movement of people and vehicles.

5. To assist those who cannot care for themselves: the intoxicated, the addicted, the mentally ill, the physically disabled, the old and the young.

6. To resolve conflict, whether it be between individuals, groups of individuals, or individuals and their government.

7. To identify problems that have the potential for becoming more serious problems for the individual citizen, for the police or for government.

8. To create and maintain a feeling of security in the community.

These multiple objectives greatly complicate the "What works?" question in policing. Which is better, for example, patrol tactic A that gets a good score for controlling serious crime, a fair score for maintaining order, and a poor score for protecting constitutional rights, or patrol tactic B that gets a good score for protecting constitutional rights, a fair score for controlling serious crime, and a poor score for maintaining order? The mere existence of these multiple objectives, and the lack of a single clear "bottom line" criterion such as profit, almost guarantees that competing strategies, programs and policies will have mixed effects that are difficult to compare and evaluate.

CONFLICTING OBJECTIVES

The multiple objectives of policing complicate the matter even further because, in some ways, they inevitably conflict with each other. To maximize orderliness in society, police would undoubtedly have to adopt methods that would endanger public satisfaction. To accomplish the greatest degree of control over serious crime, police would almost certainly have to transgress constitutional liberties. Once the pursuit of one objective detracts from the attainment of another, it is all the more difficult to derive a clear and unambiguous answer to the question, "What works?"

VAGUE OBJECTIVES

Efforts to ascertain what works in policing are also hampered by the vague character of most police objectives. Even the objective "controlling serious crime" is terribly unspecific, because "crime" includes such a vast array of illegal behaviors, many of which are regarded as serious by some segments of society. The term "serious crime" may conjure up images of violent street crime for most citizens, but some would argue for the inclusion of price-fixing, industrial pollution, and tax evasion as well. This becomes important when trying to establish "What works," for specifying the objective is a logical prerequisite to determining which practices help attain objectives and which do not.

The vagueness of police objectives also interferes with the technical tasks of measuring the state of current affairs and determining whether things are getting better or worse. Consider the objective of maintaining order in society: because it is vague, we are largely unable to measure its condition. Measuring exactly how orderly society is today seems almost impossible. How then can we know whether strategy A, that we tried last year, or strategy B, that we tried this year, "Worked better" at maintaining order? Without much opportunity to directly and reliably measure the attainment of such a vague objective, we are often left to our hunches and opinions about "what works."

LACK OF CONSENSUS

Another complication arising from the multiple objectives of policing results from the lack of consensus among citizens concerning the relative importance of each objective. Some citizens would rank the importance of "protecting constitutional rights" very near the bottom of the list of police objectives, while other citizens would rank it very near the top. Some would consider "helping those who cannot help themselves" a low-priority police objective, while others would consider it a high-priority objective. Consequently, a police strategy might "work" in the eyes of some citizens, because it contributes to the accomplishment of objectives they consider important, while other citizens would consider it an ineffective strategy, because it does not lead to the attainment of their preferred objectives.

A related lack-of-consensus problem emanates from differing standards and expectations among citizens. For example, two citizens might agree on the relative importance of the order maintenance objective, but not agree on what constitutes orderly and disorderly behavior (Wilson, 1968). One might not be bothered by a noisy party across the street, while the other might report it to the police. One might not be offended by a nearby adult bookstore while the other might be offended. Both citizens want order maintained, but they have differing views about what threatens order.

Yet another complication derives from citizens' differing views about the appropriateness of methods for accomplishing various police objectives. For example, two citizens may agree on the importance of the objective to "facilitate the safe and orderly movement of traffic" and also agree on what constitutes good and bad traffic conditions—yet they may disagree over whether police should use roadblocks and sobriety checkpoints to combat drunk driving, or radar to enforce speed limits. Similarly, citizens often disagree over whether, or at least when, police techniques such as interrogation, wiretapping, sting operations, drug courier profiling and no-knock search entries are acceptable.

COMPETING INTERESTS

Underlying many of these difficulties associated with lack of consensus and with multiple, conflicting and vague objectives is the simple but important fact that different individuals and groups in our society have different and competing interests. Ours is a *pluralistic* society in which we compete with each other for wealth, status, power and other desirable commodities. Needless to say, some individuals and groups have more advantages and more influence in this competition than do others.

Where do the police fit in this scheme? The police are one part of the system that determines the distribution of desirable commodities. When the police provide services or protection or enforce the law, they are providing advantages to some people and disadvantages to others. Now, the police can be seen as neutral ministerial agents of the criminal justice, legal, political or social service systems, as the protectors of economic elites, or as semi-autonomous agents acting with a considerable degree of freedom and discretion (Marenin, 1982). But whoever calls the shots, whoever actually controls the police and decides what strategies are employed, and which laws are given highest priority, it should be understood that police actions invariably benefit some citizens and impose costs on others.

The significance of recognizing that policing is part of our social and political system for dealing with competing interests is this—that whatever the police do supports some interests and not others. The "What works?" question, then, must to some extent be rephrased as, "What works for whom?" Consider, for example, the practice of aggressive police patrol. Evidence is presented in the first chapter of this book that aggressive patrol, including the extensive use of field interrogations and car stops, works in deterring certain kinds of serious crime. But what does it mean to say that it works? In part, it means that some people, including those who see themselves as potential victims of street muggings and thefts from autos, and those who generally favor safer streets, have their interests protected. Others, including young people, minorities and those who drive unconventional or dilapidated vehicles, will see their interests threatened by the police. Such people will be subjected to closer police surveillance and will be stopped and detained more frequently as a result of the aggressive patrol tactic. Does it "work" for them?

As another example, consider the police personnel practice of affirmative action. This practice may "work" in several respects—it may satisfy the courts that the department is doing all it can to correct past discriminatory practices, it may succeed in increasing the numbers of minorities and women in the department, and it may improve the department's reputation in some parts of the community. But at the same time, affirmative action threatens other interests, including the employment and career prospects of white males. Does affirmative action "work" for them?

The point is that the question, "What works in policing?" ultimately can be answered only within the context of an identified set of objectives and assumptions. Given that, at a particular time in a particular jurisdiction, the protection of victims against street muggings supersedes the rights of young people to walk and drive the streets unimpeded by police authority, then we can say that aggressive patrol, within the constraints established by the Constitution, works. Given that, in a particular situation, the need to correct past discrimination supersedes the interests of individual employees or applicants, we can say that affirmative action works. "What works in policing?" can be answered only in this sort of relative, contextual way, not because our knowledge about the effects of different police practices is limited (though it is), but because of the multiple, competing interests affected by the practices of the police.

CONCLUSION

As you read this book, please remember that policing and police administration often resemble a balancing act. Whether the topic is criminal investigation, domestic violence or training, we may have to ask, "Given these multiple objectives, and these competing interests, what are the most efficient and effective methods available?"

While this sounds like a much more complex and perhaps less satisfying question than simply, "What works?" one should not be overly discouraged. There has been a tremendous explosion in police research over the last 20 years, so that we do know a lot more than we used to about the effects of different police practices. In any particular decision-making or policy-making situation, a police administrator has a great deal more reliable knowledge to draw from today than was available even a decade or two ago. For practical and philosophical reasons this knowledge cannot relieve the police administrator of the ultimate responsibility for choosing among various options, but it can provide considerable help.

REFERENCES

Goldstein, H. (1977). *Policing a Free Society.* Cambridge, MA: Ballinger.

Marenin, O. (1982). "Parking Tickets and Class Repression: The Concept of Policing in Critical Theories of Criminal Justice." *Contemporary Crises,* 6,3:241-266.

Wilson, J.Q. (1968). "Dilemmas of Police Administration." *Public Administration Review,* (September-October):407-417.

Section I

POLICE OPERATIONS

Operations are those aspects of policing that involve delivery of services to the public. They include the practices that most directly affect whether the police attain their objectives or not, and the practices that most directly affect the community. Police operations are at the heart of policing.

In the opening chapter, Gary Cordner and Bob Trojanowicz discuss police patrol and general police field operations. Patrol has traditionally been the central component of police operations—it is frequently referred to as the "backbone" of policing. After describing the conventional practice of preventive patrol, the authors highlight the influential Kansas City Preventive Patrol Experiment, as well as some forms of patrol that gained popularity after the Kansas City study, such as directed patrol and foot patrol. They explain the significance of the "discovery" of fear of crime as an important police concern, especially for the resurgence of foot patrol and the growth of community policing. They also discuss the increasingly popular approach known as problem-oriented policing, pointing out both its similarities to community policing and its unique features. The authors admit their enthusiasm for community policing and problem-oriented policing, while also identifying some limitations of these promising new strategies and some unanswered questions.

The chapter on criminal investigation concentrates on reactive burglary and robbery investigations rather than on the proactive or police-initiated investigations common to vice and drug enforcement. John Eck provides an overview of the investigative process and discusses whether traditional investigative techniques help detectives solve crimes. After reviewing the important RAND study of criminal investigation which rejected the effort-result hypothesis in favor of a circumstance-result hypothesis, Eck offers an alternative triage hypothesis that rescues the police detective from the brink of extinction. This chapter summarizes and extends Eck's important *Solving Crimes* study.

In their chapter on local-level drug enforcement, Dave Hayeslip and Deborah Weisel begin with a discussion of the traditional retrospective and prospective strategies of police narcotics enforcement. Historically—due to constitutional restraints on search and seizure, corruption concerns and other factors—the role of routine patrol in drug enforcement was quite limited. However, the recent popularity of crack cocaine and its distribution through street sales has reintroduced the use of patrol saturation and sweeps for drug enforcement. Other tactics increasing in popularity include property seizure, asset forfeiture and the use of various civil remedies, such as building codes enforcement. The authors also indicate that community policing and problem-oriented policing have considerable promise for improving drug enforcement effectiveness.

In "Domestic Violence," Betsy Stanko discusses traditional and contemporary police practices for handling instances of family violence. Although in recent years many police agencies have adopted pro-arrest policies, Stanko points out that it is not at all clear whether actual police handling of domestic violence is much changed or more successful. She emphasizes the important role that police play in family violence situations, while cautioning against relying too heavily on the police to solve deep-seated personal and social problems. She suggests that while police training in handling domestic violence can still stand improvement, police departments also need to systematically reward those officers who act correctly and punish those who do not. She also advocates closer police cooperation with other agencies that address family violence, such as shelters, child protection agencies and legal aid societies.

In the final chapter in this section, Knowlton Johnson and Stephen Merker examine the effectiveness of citizen self-help measures for reducing victimization and fear of crime. Drawing on two major studies of Kentucky citizens, they conclude that self-help prevention measures are insufficient solutions to problems of fear of crime and victimization. While this research does *not* repudiate the value of such currently popular crime prevention measures as target hardening and operation identification, it does strongly suggest that police agencies should not rely exclusively or even primarily on such citizen self-help approaches to reducing crime and fear of crime.

1

Patrol

Gary W. Cordner
Eastern Kentucky University

Robert C. Trojanowicz
Michigan State University

INTRODUCTION

Since the formation of modern police forces, patrolling has been consistently recognized as the "backbone" of policing. In virtually every full-service police agency, more personnel are assigned to the patrol unit than to any other unit; in smaller agencies, the proportion of officers assigned to patrol duties can actually reach 100 percent. When police analyze their work load, they find that most of it is handled by patrol officers. When incidents occur, whether routine or emergency, patrol officers are usually the first to arrive, and thus must deal with people in the most agitated emotional conditions and confusing situations.

Although patrol may always have been the central component of policing, its nature has changed over time. After reviewing the most important of these changes, we will focus directly on the effectiveness of this mainstay of policing.

A BRIEF HISTORY

Until the early part of this century, police patrolled primarily on foot, and to a lesser extent in wagons or on horseback. They typically worked 12-hour shifts, splitting their time between their patrol beats and the station house (Uchida, 1989). Because of their geographic dispersal and the absence of communications technology, patrol officers operated largely on their own, with little supervision. They also received very little training or direction in how to perform their duties.

Much has been written about the political nature of police work in the U.S. during the 1800s. Patrol officers were more like political operatives than professional public servants (Walker, 1977). Most officers obtained their jobs through political connections, and wholesale replacements were made after each election. Corruption (Haller, 1976), brutality (Miller, 1977) and general lawlessness were widespread among police.

Just what patrol officers did in the daily conduct of their work has received less attention, but the best evidence indicates that they often did very little (Walker, 1984). Some argue that patrol officers in the 1800s employed the watchman style (Wilson, 1968), using casual and informal methods to regulate behavior on their beats according to neighborhood norms and values (Wilson & Kelling, 1982). Others consider this view to be little more than romantic nostalgia (Walker, 1984), arguing that patrol officers were unconstrained and powerful officials who frequently acted to protect personal or partisan political interests, not consensual community standards.

Clearly, patrol work changed dramatically as the twentieth century progressed. Ultimately, nearly all patrol officers were put in cars, enabling them to cover larger geographic areas and respond more rapidly to calls for service. Two-way radios were installed in patrol cars, and later became part of each officer's personal equipment, enabling direct and immediate communication between the patrol officer and the station house. Telephone service, culminating in 911 emergency systems, became almost universally available, enabling any citizen to quickly contact the police.

During this century a reform movement also changed the political nature of police work (Kelling & Moore, 1988). Employment came to depend more on merit and less on political connections. Police work became a career rather than a temporary political appointment. Educational requirements were established, and lengthy training programs were instituted. Administrative controls were implemented to minimize corruption, brutality and other abuses. The due process revolution in the courts and the civil rights movement further contributed to the reduction in police abuses of their authority (Hartmann, 1988).

An equally important development was the narrowing of the police function—or at least the narrowing of the popular image of the police function—increasingly toward crime control and law enforcement. Patrol came to be viewed in terms of the prevention and control of serious crime, as represented by the Part I crimes of the Uniform Crime Reporting system (Manning, 1977). In order to maximize the impact of patrol on crime, police began to analyze crime occurrences; allocate and deploy patrol officers in accordance with crime patterns; and emphasize one-officer cars, which were deemed more efficient than two-officer cars (Walker, 1984).

PREVENTIVE PATROL

The practice that developed is variously termed preventive patrol, interception patrol, random patrol or routine patrol. Essentially, it involves moving about (usually driving about) an assigned area in a manner designed to prevent or intercept crimes. Officers are instructed to patrol in a "systematically unsystematic" way and to avoid patrolling in predictable patterns.

Patrol officers engage in this patrolling behavior while they are free of calls for service and other assigned duties. Such time periods are often termed "free patrol time" or "uncommitted time." The amount of time available for patrolling varies greatly, of course, from one police department to another, and even from one day to the next. However, most studies have found that at least 50 percent of patrol time is uncommitted and thus available for patrolling (Whitaker, 1982).

What police officers do with their patrolling time also varies greatly—by jurisdiction, by beat, by time of day and by individual (Cordner, 1982). Patrolling can be stationary or mobile; slow-, medium- or high-speed; and oriented toward residential, commercial, recreational or other kinds of areas. Some patrol officers intervene frequently in peoples' lives by stopping cars and checking out suspicious circumstances; other officers seem more interested in inanimate matters such as parked cars and the security of closed businesses; still other officers rarely interrupt their continuous patrolling. Some officers devote all of their uncommitted time to police-related business, while others devote substantial time to loafing or personal affairs.

Presumed Effects

The widespread employment of preventive patrol has been based on the belief that it contributes to the achievement of important police objectives (Goldstein, 1977). In particular, patrol might help attain the high-priority crime control objective in two basic ways: by preventing (deterring) crime from occurring; or by intercepting crimes in progress. Patrol might also help protect people from harm and facilitate the movement of traffic (two other police objectives) in similar ways: by preventing accidents from occurring; or by intercepting dangerous driving in progress. Additionally, patrol might contribute substantially to the attainment of other police objectives by making people feel safe and secure, or by satisfying the public that the police are doing a good job.

The Evidence

Until the early 1970s, these presumed effects of police preventive patrol were largely unverified. Some tests of saturation patrolling had been conducted, but these primarily involved foot patrol (Bright, 1969; Press, 1971) or atypical settings (Chaiken, Lawless & Stevenson, 1974), and yielded inconsistent findings (see Wilson, 1975). More importantly, these tests of the effects of increased levels of patrol could not be used to firmly establish the effects of routine, preventive patrol.

During 1972 and 1973 a year-long experiment was conducted in Kansas City, Missouri to test the effects of preventive patrol (Kelling, Pate, Dieckman & Brown, 1974). The idea for the study originated within the Kansas City Police Department, and the experiment was designed and carried out with the assistance of the Police Foundation. Fifteen patrol beats were included in the study: five were control beats with normal levels of preventive patrol; five were proactive beats with 2-3 times the normal levels of patrol; and five were reactive beats, with *no* preventive patrol. It is important to realize that patrol units would enter the reactive beats to answer calls whenever requested. After handling calls, however, these patrol units would vacate the reactive beats and do their patrolling in other areas.

Before, during and after the year-long experiment, researchers measured a variety of indicators of patrol effectiveness, including reported crime, victimization, arrests, traffic accidents, fear of crime and citizen satisfaction. Their design allowed them to test two sets of questions: whether preventive patrol, as compared to no patrol, has its presumed effects; and whether extra levels of patrol have even greater effects. When the data were analyzed, no significant differences were found on any of the indicators between the control, proactive, and reactive beats. That is, neither eliminating patrol nor adding extra patrol for one year in the experimental area in Kansas City had any effects on reported crime, victimization, arrests, traffic citations, fear of crime, or citizen satisfaction. In fact, interviews indicated that the citizens of Kansas City, including those residents of the five reactive beats in which patrol had been eliminated, failed to even notice that levels of police patrol had been altered.

To this day, many people carelessly over-interpret the findings of the Kansas City study. The study did not prove that police have no effect on crime; that police forces should be reduced in size; that patrol can be eliminated indefinitely; or that all levels of patrol saturation are ineffective. Rather, the study demonstrated that varying the level of motorized patrol between zero cars per beat and 2-3 cars per beat, for one year in one city, had no effect. Yet even this more modest statement of the study's findings is dramatically important, because until Kansas City the assumption had been that motorized preventive patrol was absolutely crucial and that it had to be maintained at all costs. After Kansas City, it became feasible to consider reallocating at least some of the substantial police resources devoted to preventive patrol.

RELATED RESEARCH

The Kansas City study stands out as *the* authoritative test of the effects of police patrol. A number of other, less rigorous or more narrowly focused studies, though, have produced useful information about important aspects of patrol effectiveness.

Directed Patrol

An obvious alternative to self-directed, random, "systematically unsystematic" patrol is the strategy now called *directed patrol*. Under this strategy, patrol officers are directed to spend some of their patrol time in certain areas, to adopt certain tactics, and/or to watch for certain kinds of offenses. These directions are usually based on crime analysis information. Some departments have chosen to replace routine preventive patrol largely with directed patrol, while other departments use directed patrol only sporadically.

The available evidence indicates that the use of directed patrol can reduce the incidence of target crimes (such as street robberies or larcenies from autos) in target areas (Cordner, 1981). However, diminishing returns seem to set in with the extensive utilization of directed patrol. More importantly, whether directed patrol prevents crime or merely displaces it is not known, nor is it clear whether directed patrol is any more effective than other alternative strategies. Stronger evidence may soon be available from a major directed patrol study just completed in Minneapolis (Sherman, 1990a).

Saturation Patrol

Studies of the effects of saturating areas with high levels of patrol have yielded mixed results. Doubling foot patrols in New York seemed to reduce crime (Wilson, 1975); in England, however, increasing foot patrols from one to two officers per beat had no effect on crime, although further increases did reduce crime (Bright, 1969). Increased nighttime patrols in the New York subways decreased crime substantially; however, the incidence of crime on the subways increased concomitantly during the daytime (Chaiken et al., 1974). Studies in Nashville suggested that heavy saturation of motorized patrol during the daytime failed to reduce crime but that similar saturation during nighttime hours did decrease crime (Schnelle, Kirchner, McNees & Lawler, 1975; Schnelle, Kirchner, Casey, Uselton & McNees, 1977).

Aggressive Patrol

Several studies consistently have found that *aggressive patrol,* which involves a high level of patrol intervention through traffic stops and checking out suspicious people on the street, reduces the incidence of street crimes. In an experimental test in San Diego, eliminating the use of field interrogations (FIs) led to crime increases, whereas reinstituting FIs resulted in crime decreases (Boydstun, 1975). Two cross-sectional studies found that cities with more aggressive patrol tactics had lower robbery rates (Wilson & Boland, 1976; 1979). And the crime reduction effects of directed patrol seem to result more from frequent traffic stops and FIs in target areas than simply from increased patrolling time in such areas (Cordner, 1981).

It should be recognized that aggressive patrol may have deleterious effects on citizen satisfaction with the police. The increased level of police interventions may not always be appreciated, especially by those people who are stopped and temporarily detained. Such dissatisfaction may be minimized if police are skillful in picking out truly suspicious people and in persuading people of the legitimacy of aggressive police actions (Boydstun, 1975), but with more interventions more complaints would seem inevitable.

Sherman (1990b) has recently pointed out that police saturation and aggressive patrol are often combined with media publicity in the form of crackdowns. These *crackdowns* are popular strategies for dealing with such problems as street-level drug sales, prostitution, and driving while intoxicated. While the independent effects of saturation, aggressive tactics, and publicity are difficult to separate, there is evidence that crackdowns have both immediate and residual deterrent value. The possibility of residual deterrence suggests that if police could become adept at timing their crackdowns, they could "leave behind" some deterrent effects as they move on to the next problem location or target offense.

Foot Patrol

Although some evidence has been gathered to support the limited effectiveness of directed patrol, saturation patrol, aggressive patrol, and crackdowns, the overall demoralizing results of the Kansas City Preventive Patrol Experiment have come to pervade much of our thinking about police patrol. Little empirical support can be identified for having patrol officers spend three to five hours each shift riding around in their cars. Even the rationale that patrol officers must be riding around "doing nothing" in order to be immediately available to respond to calls for service has been challenged. Studies of police response time (Spelman & Brown, 1981) and differential response strategies (McEwen, Connors & Cohen, 1986), surprisingly, have indicated that rapid response is necessary for only a small subset of all reported crimes and other incidents.

By the early 1980s, the cumulative effects of studies of preventive patrol, response time, and follow-up criminal investigations by detectives (Greenwood & Petersilia, 1975) had created a sense that "nothing worked" in policing. Ironically, the first major studies to reverse this trend were focused on a once-popular police strategy that had been all but discarded in the modern era—foot patrol. Although several tests of foot patrol effectiveness had been conducted in the 1960s and 1970s, the most important studies, with very interesting results, were conducted more recently in Newark, New Jersey (Police Foundation, 1981) and Flint, Michigan (Trojanowicz, 1982).

In Newark, three sets of foot patrol beats were experimentally manipulated: beats that already had foot patrol and retained it; beats from which existing foot patrol was removed; and beats without foot patrol that had it added for the course of the study. Similar to the Kansas City study of motorized patrol, researchers in Newark measured reported crime, victimization, arrests, fear, and citizen satisfaction before and after the experimental period.

Consistent with the findings from Kansas City for motorized patrol, foot patrol in Newark was found to have little or no effect on crime. However, citizens in Newark noticed the presence or absence of foot patrol in their neighborhoods; they were more satisfied with police service if served by foot patrol; and the presence of foot patrol seemed to lead to decreased levels of fear of crime. These positive effects of foot patrol stood in stark contrast to the finding of "no effects" for motorized patrol in Kansas City.

In Flint, the introduction of foot patrol was not only associated with decreased citizen fear of crime and increased citizen satisfaction with police, but also with crime and call for service decreases. The foot patrols became so popular that citizens in the fiscally strapped city voted three times for special tax increases to maintain and expand the program.

What made the foot patrol research so influential were two related developments: the "discovery" of fear of crime as a major social problem and legitimate focus of police attention and resources; and interpretations of the foot patrol findings that led to the development of community policing programs around the country.

FEAR OF CRIME

The scope of the fear of crime problem has only recently been appreciated. According to the *Figgie Report* on fear of crime (Research & Forecasts, 1982), four of every ten Americans express a serious fear of crime. In the same report's 14-city profile, a survey of 500 residents of Detroit found more than half expressing serious concern about becoming a victim of a major crime. A random sample of 1,000 Texas residents showed that 57 percent worried they would become victims of serious crimes in the next year, and half said they were afraid to walk within a mile of their homes at night (Teske & Powell, 1978). As the editor of *Harper's* magazine expressed it, "The nation spends at least $40 billion a year for the various forms of police protection, but nobody feels safe" (Lapham, 1985:40).

Police awareness of the magnitude of citizen fears has been coupled with the recognition that fear of crime is more than simply a direct manifestation of the actual amount of crime (Furstenberg, 1972; DuBow, McCabe & Kaplan, 1979; Skogan & Maxfield, 1981). The most fearful individuals often are *not* those who have been personally victimized or those whose places of residence or lifestyles make them most susceptible to criminal victimization. Similarly, fear of crime often increases even though the level of crime is steady or decreasing. Individual and collective fear is influenced by a wide variety of factors, including sex, age, race, feelings of personal vulnerability, the experiences of friends and relatives, media presentations, community cohesion, and patterns of neighborhood decline and rejuvenation.

Since fear is a major problem in its own right, and not merely a reflection of actual crime conditions, it follows that efforts directed specifically at fear-reduction might be appropriate (Moore & Trojanowicz, 1988). Police strategists and administrators came to this realization at about the same time that the Newark and Flint studies revealed that foot patrol helped reduce citizen fear. The subsequent adoption of foot patrol aimed primarily at fear-reduction was further legitimized by the general lack of evidence in support of any other police strategies aimed at reducing crime itself—at least foot patrol could be shown to affect *something*.

COMMUNITY POLICING

When police scholars set out to explain the results of the Newark foot patrol study, which showed that fear and citizen satisfaction were improved even though crime was unaffected, they provided a major boost to the development of community policing. One explanation focused on the sense of personal presence that is created by foot patrol. Certainly some citizens, and perhaps most, value the informal, personal contact with foot patrol officers that is not often made available by motor patrol officers. The effects of something as simple as letting citizens get to know their patrol officers by name and by sight perhaps should not be underestimated.

Wilson and Kelling (1982) substantially extended the rationale behind foot patrol with their "broken windows" argument. In their view, foot patrol officers are much more likely than motor patrol officers to attend to "soft crime" and public order problems on their own initiative. The foot patrol officer is less likely than the motor patrol officer to ignore panhandlers, for example—exposure is more intimate and of longer duration for the officer walking past the panhandler than for the officer driving past, it is harder to pretend to have not seen the problem or to claim to be on the way to a more serious incident, citizen pressure to intervene is more immediate, etc. This increased foot patrol intervention in such relatively minor matters can be significant because substantial citizen fear is caused by unruly youths, abandoned cars, noisy radios, and similar "signs of crime." Wilson and Kelling argue that it is foot patrol's attention to these signs of crime that accounts for much of its fear-reduction effect, and further that such attention can help bolster neighborhoods and prevent decline and decay.

During the last decade, initial interest in foot patrol has broadened and deepened into widespread enthusiasm for community policing (Kelling, 1988; Trojanowicz & Bucqueroux, 1990). In addition to the research and developments already described, several other factors have combined to fuel this enthusiasm: a desire to capture the benefits of foot patrol even in communities where foot patrol is not feasible; parallel developments in crime prevention programming that increasingly emphasized police and community co-production of public safety; a desire in some quarters to replace legalistic and/or bureaucratic styles of policing; and a desire to decentralize large police organizations. Most recently, close cooperation between police officers and the community has been identified as one of the more promising strategies for reducing drug-related problems (Moore & Kleiman, 1989).

Community policing can take the form of a philosophy and set of values for guiding a police department, it can be a department-wide strategy, and/or it can include specific programs and tactics. Because of its broad parameters, community policing can take many different forms, and in fact does vary greatly in the hundreds of police departments currently implementing it in one fashion or another. Some agencies have special units doing community policing, while others ask all officers to incorporate it into their day-to-day activities. Among the more popular community policing programs and tactics are permanent beat assignments, foot patrol, park-and-walk, storefront centers, neighborhood watch, door-to-door policing, police athletic leagues, and community newsletters.

In most departments, community policing is not intended to completely substitute for motor patrol, but rather to supplement and complement motor patrol's reactive efforts. Calls for service, including emergencies, still need to be answered, whether by community-based officers or by a mobile response force. Some of the departments most serious about implementing community policing, though, have adopted call screening procedures and differential responses policies designed to: (1) handle information requests and minor report-taking over the telephone; (2) minimize as much as possible the need for immediate mobile responses to calls; (3) minimize cross-beat dispatching; and (4) increase the portion of calls that are assigned to community-based officers (i.e., to maximize the extent to which they monopolize the delivery of police services in their assigned communities).

In its various forms, community policing universally seeks closer and more productive contact between officers and area residents. Over and above the fear-reduction and public satisfaction benefits of such contact, the unique information obtained by officers from citizens and from personal observations can be of tremendous value. For example, in Flint, motor patrol officers had staked out the home of an armed robbery suspect when the foot patrol officer arrived. Not only did the foot officer provide the suspect's name and description, he also told the other officers that the suspect drank heavily, and that when he did, the suspect's wife usually went to her sister's home. When the officers called the sister, they learned that the suspect's wife and children were in fact there at the sister's house, and that the suspect was home in his bedroom, drunk. This information allowed the officers to safely raid the home and arrest the suspect without incident.

Similarly, in New York, when a community police officer (CPO) read the descriptions of three rapists who had been attacking women on her beat, something triggered her memory. She followed up her hunch by contacting the Sex Crimes Unit, and later when she spotted the suspects on the street, she arrested them herself. Another New York CPO drew on his beat knowledge to unravel a series of stolen check cases—he was the only person in a position to realize that the several victimized businesses all used the same cash register repairman, who turned out to be the culprit.

These vignettes illustrate the kinds of crime-fighting benefits that can accrue to police officers as a result of closer contact with the community. Taken together with police-community relations benefits and fear-reduction effects, they demonstrate the potential value of community policing. Because community policing incorporates such a diverse range of tactics, strategies, and programs, however, we have so far had little authoritative empirical research beyond the foot patrol studies. One major study did look at efforts to reduce fear in Houston and Newark (Pate, Wycoff, Skogan & Sherman, 1986), with mixed and somewhat inconclusive findings. In that study, though, it was determined that the more successful programmatic elements of community policing were those that (1) provided time for police-citizen interaction and (2) relied on police officer initiative in responding to citizen concerns. Studies currently underway in Aurora, Colorado; Alexandria, Virginia; and McAllen, Texas may help identify more clearly the specific effects of community policing.

PROBLEM-ORIENTED POLICING

A concept that complements community policing, and that has been developing both in conjunction with community policing and separately, is problem-oriented policing. This concept was originated by Herman Goldstein (1979; 1990; see also Wilson & Kelling, 1989) and had its most important tests in Newport News, Virginia (Eck & Spelman, 1987a; 1987b) and in Baltimore County, Maryland (Cordner, 1986; Taft, 1986).

Problem-oriented policing is based on several principles that seem only a matter of common sense, but which may not characterize modern policing as it has evolved over the years. These include identifying persistent community problems, gathering diverse data to identify and analyze such problems, and considering a wide variety of problem solutions. Arguably, modern policing rarely follows this pattern; rather, each call for service is treated as if it is unconnected to all other matters, only limited data is gathered from complainants and witnesses, and only a few alternatives (such as do nothing, warn, or arrest) are ever considered. Modern policing can thus best be called incident-driven, or single-complaint policing, as contrasted with problem-oriented policing.

In Newport News, efforts were made to implement problem-oriented policing department-wide. Officers and supervisors were encouraged to identify persistent problems in their beats, or facing their units, and then to use problem-solving techniques to address them. Some projects resulted in substantial target crime decreases, while others reported similar successes in reducing other kinds of problems. For example, an officer who had identified a recurring weekend-night problem involving noisy youths determined that the youths were walking home from a skating rink after its closing. The youths rode a city transit bus to the rink, but the bus stopped running before the rink closed for the night. The officer was able to convince the transit system to keep the bus in service a little later on weekend nights, and the problem was resolved.

In Baltimore County, problem-oriented policing was adopted primarily in an effort to reduce fear of crime. A special unit (COPE—Citizen Oriented Police Enforcement) had been created in 1982 with a fear-reduction mission. Interestingly, the unit first implemented saturation patrol tactics, and then evolved into a community- and problem-oriented strategy. As it evolved, its effects on fear became more substantial. The COPE unit eventually adopted a process of problem-oriented policing that included heavy reliance on citizen input to problem identification and citizen participation in problem resolution. This combination of community policing and problem-oriented policing seems to offer one of our brightest prospects for improved police effectiveness.

CONCLUSION

The available research leads inevitably to the conclusion that traditional mobile patrol has little impact on crime, fear of crime, or other major police objectives; that such refinements as directed patrol, saturation patrol, and aggressive patrol have at least some limited effects on the incidence of street crimes; and that foot patrol and community policing have beneficial effects on fear of crime and citizen satisfaction with police. The available evidence also seems to clearly demonstrate that problem-oriented policing contributes to more effective police problem solving—but because these problems may be related to crime, fear, or a wide variety of other matters, broader generalizations are difficult to offer.

There is a great deal yet to be determined about the effectiveness of these various strategies and tactics, however, and there are also important costs and questions that should temper our enthusiasm for community- and problem-oriented policing (Manning, 1984; Goldstein, 1987; Greene & Mastrofski, 1988; Riechers & Roberg, 1990). A few of the most important questions and issues are identified below.

1. At its heart, community policing advocates policing in accordance with the norms and values of each separate community. How much differentiation in police practices is desirable? Will such differentiation inevitably favor insiders over outsiders?

2. In order to be responsive under community policing, police have to be able to identify what the community wants. How do the police resolve conflicting demands from community interests? What if the community is apathetic? What if no "community" exists at all?

3. As part of community and problem-oriented policing, police often become self-appointed advocates for community

improvement. Do we want the police to assume such political roles? How will conflicts with elected politicians and appointed officials be resolved?

4. In community and problem-oriented policing, the police often seem to emphasize fear-reduction, citizen satisfaction, and general-purpose problem solving over crime fighting. Should the police be marketing these other services or concentrating on improving their success in accomplishing their crime control mission?

5. Community and problem-oriented policing are time-intensive strategies. Can the police implement them and still meet their other responsibilities, including call-handling, emergency response, and follow-up criminal investigations? Particularly in large cities, where the problems are most severe and communities are most disaffected, are community and problem-oriented policing really feasible alternatives?

Despite these difficult and largely unanswered questions, much has been learned in the last two decades about what works (and what does not work) in police patrol. An atmosphere conducive to experimentation and further learning exists in many police departments today, giving reason for even more optimism about improved patrol productivity in the years to come.

REFERENCES

Boydstun, J.E. (1975). *San Diego Field Interrogation: Final Report.* Washington, DC: Police Foundation.

Bright, J.A. (1969). *Beat Patrol Experiment.* London: Home Office.

Chaiken, J.M., M.W. Lawless & K.A. Stevenson (1974). *The Impact of Police Activity on Crime: Robberies in the New York City Subway System.* New York: Rand Institute.

Cordner, G.W. (1981). "The Effects of Directed Patrol: A Natural Quasi-Experiment in Pontiac." In J.J. Fyfe (ed.) *Contemporary Issues in Law Enforcement,* pp. 37-58. Beverly Hills, CA: Sage Publications.

_____ (1982). "While on Routine Patrol: What the Police Do When They're Not Doing Anything." *American Journal of Police,* 1,2:94-112.

_____ (1986). "Fear of Crime and the Police: An Evaluation of a Fear-Reduction Strategy." *Journal of Police Science and Administration,* 14,3:223-233.

Dubow, F., E. McCabe & G. Kaplan (1979). *Reactions to Crime: A Critical Review of the Literature.* Washington, DC: Government Printing Office.

Eck, J.E. & W. Spelman (1987a). *Problem Solving: Problem-Oriented Policing in Newport News.* Washington, DC: Police Executive Research Forum.

_____ (1987b). "Who Ya Gonna Call? The Police as Problem Busters." *Crime & Delinquency,* 33,1(January):31-52.

Furstenberg, F.F., Jr. (1972). "Fear of Crime and Its Effects on Citizen Behavior." In A. Biderman (ed.) *Crime and Justice: A Symposium.* New York: Nailburg.

Goldstein, H. (1977). *Policing a Free Society.* Cambridge, MA: Ballinger.

_____ (1979). "Improving Policing: A Problem-Oriented Approach." *Crime & Delinquency,* 25:236-258.

_____ (1987). "Toward Community-Oriented Policing: Potential, Basic Requirements, and Threshold Questions." *Crime & Delinquency,* 33,1(January):6-30.

_____ (1990). *Problem-Oriented Policing.* New York: McGraw-Hill.

Greene, J.R. & S. Mastrofski (eds.) (1988). *Community Policing: Rhetoric or Reality.* New York: Praeger.

Greenwood, P.W. & J. Petersilia (1975). *The Criminal Investigation Process Volume I: Summary and Policy Implications.* Santa Monica, CA: RAND Corporation.

Haller, M. (1976). "Historical Roots of Police Behavior: Chicago, 1890-1925." *Law and Society Review,* 10(Winter):303-324.

Hartmann, F.X. (1988). "Debating the Evolution of American Policing." *Perspectives on Policing.* Washington, DC: National Institute of Justice.

Kelling, G.L. (1988). "Police and Communities: The Quiet Revolution." *Perspectives on Policing.* Washington, DC: National Institute of Justice.

_____ ,T. Pate, D. Dieckman & C.E. Brown (1974). *The Kansas City Preventive Patrol Experiment: A Summary Report.* Washington, DC: Police Foundation.

_____ & M.H. Moore (1988). "The Evolving Strategy of Policing." *Perspectives on Policing.* Washington, DC: National Institute of Justice.

Lapham, L. (1985). "Images of Fear." *Harper's* (May).

Manning, P.K. (1977). *Police Work: The Social Organization of Policing.* Cambridge, MA: MIT Press.

_____ (1984). "Community Policing." *American Journal of Police,* 3,2:205-227.

McEwen, J.T., E.F. Connors & M.I. Cohen (1986). *Evaluation of the Differential Police Response Field Test*. Washington, DC: National Institute of Justice.

Miller, W.R. (1977). *Cops and Bobbies: Police Authority in New York and London, 1830-1870*. Chicago: University of Chicago Press.

Moore, M.M. & R.C. Trojanowicz (1988). "Policing and the Fear of Crime." *Perspectives on Policing*. Washington, DC: National Institute of Justice.

Moore, M.M. & M.A.R. Kleiman (1989). "The Police and Drugs." *Perspectives on Policing*. Washington, DC: National Institute of Justice.

Pate, A.M., M.A. Wycoff, L.W. Sherman & W.G. Skogan (1986). *Reducing Fear of Crime in Houston and Newark: A Summary Report*. Washington, DC: Police Foundation.

Police Foundation (1981). *The Newark Foot Patrol Experiment*. Washington, DC: Police Foundation.

Press, S.J. (1971). *Some Effects of an Increase in Police Manpower in the 20th Precinct of New York City*. New York: Rand Institute.

Research and Forecasts, Inc. (1982). *The Figgie Report on Fear of Crime*. Willoughby, OH: Figgie International, Inc.

Riechers, L.M. & R.R. Roberg (1990). "Community Policing: A Critical Review of Underlying Assumptions." *Journal of Police Science and Administration* 17,2(June):105-114.

Schnelle, J.F., R.E. Kirchner, M.P. McNees & J.M. Lawler (1975). "Social Evaluation Research: The Evaluation of Two Police Patrolling Strategies." *Journal of Applied Behavior Analysis*, 8(Winter).

Schnelle, J.F., R.E. Kirchner, J.D. Casey, P.H. Uselton, Jr. & M.P. McNees (1977). "Patrol Evaluation Research: A Multiple-Baseline Analysis of Saturation Police Patrolling During Day and Night Hours." *Journal of Applied Behavior Analysis*, 10(Spring).

Sherman, L.W. (1990a). Plenary session presentation, Academy of Criminal Justice Sciences annual meeting, Denver, March.

_____ (1990b). "Police Crackdowns." *NIJ Reports*, (March/April):2-6.

Skogan, W.G. & M.G. Maxfield (1981). *Coping with Crime: Individual and Neighborhood Reactions*. Beverly Hills, CA: Sage Publications.

Spelman, W. & D.K. Brown (1981). *Calling the Police: Citizen Reporting of Serious Crime*. Washington, DC: Police Executive Research Forum.

Taft, P.B., Jr. (1986). *Fighting Fear: The Baltimore County COPE Project.* Washington, DC: Police Executive Research Forum.

Teske, R.H.C., Jr. & N.L. Powell (1978). *Texas Crime Poll: Spring 1978 Survey.* Huntsville, TX: Criminal Justice Center, Sam Houston State University.

Trojanowicz, R. (1982). *An Evaluation of the Neighborhood Foot Patrol Program in Flint, Michigan.* East Lansing, MI: National Center for Community Policing, Michigan State University.

_____ & B. Bucqueroux (1990). *Community Policing: A Contemporary Perspective.* Cincinnati, OH: Anderson Publishing Co.

Uchida, C.D. (1989). "The Development of the American Police: An Historical Overview." In R.G. Dunham & G.P. Alpert (eds.) *Critical Issues in Policing: Contemporary Readings*, pp. 14-30. Prospect Heights, IL: Waveland Press.

Walker, S. (1977). *A Critical History of Police Reform: The Emergence of Professionalism.* Lexington, MA: D.C. Heath.

_____ (1984). "Broken Windows and Fractured History: The Use and Misuse of History in Recent Police Patrol Analysis." *Justice Quarterly,* 1,1:75-90.

Whitaker, G.P. (1982). "What is Patrol Work?" *Police Studies* 4:13-22.

Wilson, J.Q. (1968). *Varieties of Police Behavior: The Management of Law and Order in Eight Communities.* Cambridge, MA: Harvard University Press.

_____ (1975). *Thinking About Crime.* New York: Basic Books.

_____ & B. Boland (1976). "Crime." In W. Gorham & N. Glazer (eds.) *The Urban Predicament.* Washington, DC: Urban Institute.

_____ & B. Boland (1979). *The Effect of the Police on Crime.* Washington, DC: U.S. Government Printing Office.

_____ & G.L. Kelling (1982). "Police and Neighborhood Safety: Broken Windows." *Atlantic Monthly,* (March):29-38.

_____ & G.L. Kelling (1989). "Making Neighborhoods Safe." *Atlantic Monthly,* (February):46-52.

2

Criminal Investigation

John E. Eck
Police Executive Research Forum

INTRODUCTION

Police investigations can inspire fear, awe, security, suspense, and mystery. They have been the subject of countless novels, innumerable movies and too many television plots. For many, police work is virtually synonymous with investigations. But despite our fascination with the subject, most of what we know comes from detective experience and literary and media myths. Over the past 20 years, research has begun to shed some light on investigations, illuminating general shapes. We are now beginning to see some of the detail as further research focuses more closely on earlier findings.

Still, the commonly held picture of detectives' work is that it involves sleuthing out clues in sordid underworld dens, deductive reasoning based on speedy and accurate lab work and intuition, and nearly always apprehending the criminal. Yet early research showed that detective work is often boring, usually requires only normal decision-making powers, and seldom leads to solutions. The reason for these findings is that most crimes betray scant leads.

The early research and the public myth are equally interesting and may be equally misleading. More recent research has shown that investigative work is neither as inspiring as the public may believe nor as fruitless as the first research suggested.

Early research on police investigations addressed the issues of detective effectiveness and productivity. It focused on the question: Does detective investigative work help solve crimes? This is also the question addressed in this chapter. Two rival hypotheses attempt to answer the question, each plausible and each based on some evidence. We will review these hypotheses and their supporting evidence and then suggest a third hypothesis which more accurately fits the data.

This chapter concentrates on reactive investigations of crimes. These are investigations that begin when a citizen reports an offense against a victim. Most information describing reactive investigations comes from studies of burglary and robbery investigations. Thus, generalizing findings to all reactive investigations may be problematic. Police officers also engage in proactive or police-initiated investigations of criminals. These types of investigations are common to vice and drug enforcement, but they are not the subject of this chapter.

Before we address the main question, we will describe the investigative process. Once we have set the stage, we will move on to the main question.

THE INVESTIGATIVE PROCESS

Larger police agencies in the United States usually divide the investigative function between a patrol division and an investigative division. However, other units such as records, communications, administration, and special services also contribute to investigations. Because investigative units are the only portion of most police agencies that are almost totally devoted to investigative work, detectives are central to the investigative function. The patrol division is the single biggest component of any full-service law enforcement agency, comprising almost 50 percent of the officers. But patrol officers spend much of their time on non-crime-related activities. Investigative units include only 10 percent of the typical agency's officers, but the detectives in these units are almost totally engaged in investigative or related activities (Police Executive Research Forum, 1981).

Until recently, the role of patrol officers in investigations was to serve as report takers. They took statements from victims to establish that a crime occurred, but did little other probing. After they took a report the case was given to a detective for completion of the investigative work. In some agencies (and it is impossible to determine how many) patrol officers still have only such a limited role in investigations. This is changing, however, as police agencies assign more investigative duties, for a wider variety of offenses, to patrol officers. In many agencies, patrol officers investigate all misdemeanors. In other agencies patrol officers handle investigations of felonies such as burglary and larceny. But even in agencies where patrol officers have a major role in investigating offenses, detectives still handle the most serious and complex cases.

Still, most large police agencies split the responsibility for the investigation of felonies between the patrol and detective divisions. The patrol officer handles the initial stage of the investigation, often called the preliminary investigation. Detectives handle any further, follow-up investigation.

Figure 2.1 shows the types of activities patrol officers engage in during preliminary investigations of burglaries and robberies. This information comes from logs completed by patrol officers in three police agencies—the Dekalb County (GA) Police Department, the St. Petersburg (FL) Police Department, and the Wichita (KS) Police Department (Eck, 1983). Later we will say more about the study that collected this information. Figure 2.1 shows that interviewing victims and checking crime scenes are the two most common activities, performed in over 90 percent of the cases. Patrol officers take all other actions in less than half the cases.

Figure 2.1
PATROL INVESTIGATIVE ACTIVITIES
percent of cases by crime type

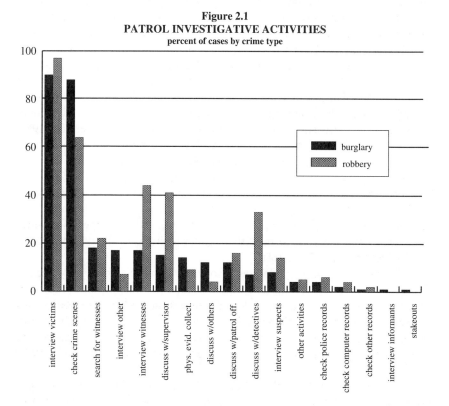

Preliminary investigation for burglaries seems to be largely a matter of report taking. Officers interview victims and check the crime scenes in virtually all burglaries. But they infrequently search for and talk to witnesses, check files, talk to informants, or interview suspects. This pattern of activities may be because other activities are often inappropriate. Burglary is normally a crime of stealth. Burglars seek to avoid being detected by victims and witnesses. Therefore officers usually have few clues upon which to base an investigation.

Robbers are more blatant. By definition, the offender and the victim must interact. Though this does not guarantee that the victim is a witness—an elderly woman who has been knocked down from behind and has had her purse taken may have seen nothing of the attacker—it does increase the chances that the victim will be able to describe the offender. Further, robberies occurring in public settings, like the holdup of a convenience store or the mugging in a parking lot, are more likely to be witnessed by third parties than burglaries.

So it is not surprising that robberies are handled a bit differently than burglaries. Officers are more likely to interview witnesses in robbery investigations, and patrol officers are more likely to discuss robbery cases with supervisors, detectives, and other patrol officers than burglary cases.

Once a patrol officer has completed a preliminary investigation, someone needs to decide whether to continue the investigation. In the past, the absence of a police policy left this decision to the detective who received the case. The absence of a policy also meant that detectives followed no formal criteria when making this decision. Over the past decade, police agencies have increasingly adopted formal case screening rules. By 1981, over 83 percent of the agencies serving 50,000 or more people used some form of case screening (Police Executive Research Forum, 1981).

Police agencies use a variety of screening procedures. Some agencies provide guidelines for patrol officers or patrol supervisors to use when screening cases. A more common method is to have case screening conducted by an investigative supervisor. Guidelines tell the supervisor which cases they should assign to detectives and which cases should not receive any further investigative effort.

The case screening guidelines also vary. Some agencies only suggest the clues the screener should take into account when making such decisions. These guidelines allow a great deal of discretion. Others are statistically derived lists of clues with numerical weights that allow little discretion. These clues include information that may result in suspect identification and arrest, describe crime seriousness, or specify the crime type (Eck, 1979; Gaines et al., 1983).

Few researchers have described what detectives do during investigations. Greenwood et al. (1977) demonstrated that detective actions relating to the solution of crimes are most often standard police procedures and not the strange and fantastic actions of the detective mythology. Although true, Greenwood et al. only looked at solved crimes. Since detectives solve few crimes their study provided a distorted picture of the importance of the actions taken by detectives.

Figure 2.2 shows the frequency of actions taken by detectives during follow-up investigations of burglaries and robberies. The information came from logs completed by detectives investigating these offenses at three jurisdictions (Eck, 1983). The most common activity is the victim interview. No other activity is particularly common. This suggests that the pattern of activities conducted by detectives varies from offense to offense, depending on the nature of the leads available. Though burglary and robbery follow-up investigations display similar activity patterns, almost all detective activities are more common for robberies than burglaries.

Since cases have varying numbers of clues, investigations are not all the same length. Above, we discussed how case screening is used to curtail investigations. But even if a case is assigned to a detective, it may not remain active for very long. Promising leads do not always pan out. Alternatively, a suspect identified to the patrol officer may be arrested a few days later by a detective.

Figure 2.2
DETECTIVE INVESTIGATIVE ACTIVITIES
percent of cases by crime type

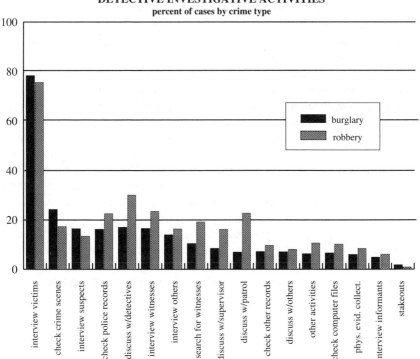

As Figure 2.3 demonstrates, the vast majority of investigations of burglaries and robberies are over by the third investigation day (after a day for
the preliminary investigation, and two days for the follow-up). Almost half
of the burglaries have been screened out by the second investigation day.
Since none of the three agencies screened robberies, all were being
actively investigated by the second investigation day when the follow-up
began. Nevertheless, by day three the proportion of robberies still being
investigated is only slightly higher than the proportion of active burglary
cases. On subsequent investigation days the difference narrows still further.
This rapid attrition of cases is consistent with the findings of Bynum et al.
(1982) that detectives did not put much effort into 82 percent of the cases
they handled.

Indeed, when we organized these actions by the investigation day on
which they occurred we found that the longer the investigations were active,
the more diverse the actions became. On the first follow-up investigation
day, victim interviews and crime scene checks predominated. The focus of
the investigation at this early stage is on information sources outside departmental control, such as victims, witnesses, and crime scenes. By the third
and later follow-up investigation days, there is no action that predominates.
The detectives direct the most frequent activities at information sources
within departmental control, such as records, other detectives, patrol officers, and suspects (Eck, 1983).

Investigations become less victim-oriented and more suspect-oriented
as time passes. The proportion of active cases involving a victim interview
during an investigation day declines, as the proportion of cases involving a
suspect interview increases. This process, illustrated in Figures 2.4 and 2.5,
is in part due to the attrition of cases (profiled in Figure 2.3) with exhausted
leads. This also occurs because the leads in the remaining, more promising
cases force detectives to take a variety of actions. These leads point to suspects, so investigative actions, while becoming more diverse, also become
more suspect-oriented. Sources of information within the control of the
department become more important as detectives check early leads. Victims
become less important (unless they actually witnessed the offense) because
they have little to contribute after detectives have interviewed them early in
the investigation. Thus, we can draw a portrait of how investigations
progress, despite the absence of a typical pattern of specific actions.

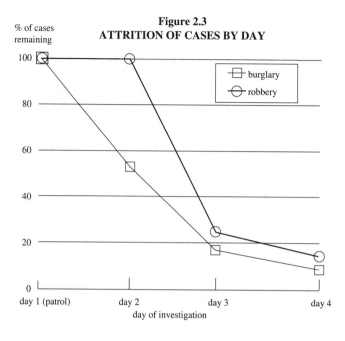

Figure 2.3
ATTRITION OF CASES BY DAY

% of cases remaining

legend: burglary, robbery

day 1 (patrol)   day 2   day 3   day 4

day of investigation

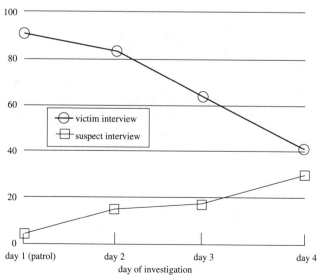

Figure 2.4
ACTIVITIES BY DAY OF INVESTIGATION
OF BURGLARIES

% of cases with activity

legend: victim interview, suspect interview

day 1 (patrol)   day 2   day 3   day 4

day of investigation

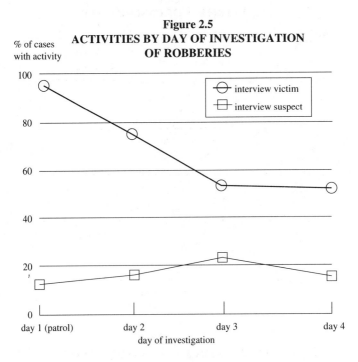

Figure 2.5
ACTIVITIES BY DAY OF INVESTIGATION
OF ROBBERIES

SOLVING CRIMES

Does all of this effort make a difference? Researchers have paid considerable attention to the productivity of investigations. They have been particularly concerned with how investigators solve crimes and the relative contributions of patrol officers and detectives. Based on earlier research, two apparently contradictory hypotheses can be discerned.

The first suggests that investigative results, such as arrests, are beyond police control. Random circumstances—the presence of a witness, whether the victim had marked his stolen property, the presence of physical evidence, and the ability of the victim to identify a suspect—dictate case outcomes. If the circumstances are not favorable, then an investigator cannot make an arrest. Under favorable circumstances, an investigator can make an arrest. The role of the patrol officer is critical because he or she determines whether the necessary leads are present and, as a consequence, whether conditions are favorable for an arrest. Detectives process the case and complete the paper work. They pick up and interrogate suspects identified during preliminary investigations and prepare cases for prosecution. Little investigative work (in the normal meaning of the term) is performed. Peter Greenwood has been the most articulate spokesman for this *circumstance-result* hypothesis.

> [The] solution of any particular property crime is a chance event, insensitive to the amount of investigation conducted (Greenwood, 1970:37).

> On how cases are solved: The single most important determinant of whether or not a case will be solved is the information the victim supplies to the immediately responding patrol officer. If information that uniquely identifies the perpetrator is not presented at the time the crime is reported, the perpetrator, by and large, will not be subsequently identified (Greenwood & Petersilia, 1975:vii).

Studies by Isaacs (1967), Greenwood (1970), Greenwood et al. (1977), Eck (1979), and Gaines et al. (1983) support the circumstance-result hypothesis. Among police researchers, during the past decade, this description of how crimes are solved has become the dominant hypothesis.

The evidence supporting it is not conclusive, however. Isaacs (1967) used highly aggregated data, comprised of many offenses. Further, he did not measure the effort of investigators, nor did he describe what they did to solve offenses. Greenwood (1970) used precinct-level data. Though he separately analyzed burglaries and assaults, he did not collect information on case characteristics and investigators' efforts. The study by Greenwood et al. (1977) looked at cleared cases only. This made it impossible to determine the factors that discriminate between cases that did and did not result in an arrest. Finally, Greenberg et al. (1973), Greenberg et al. (1975), Eck (1979), and Gaines et al. (1983) did not collect data on what detectives did after the preliminary investigation. As a result, none of the studies supporting the circumstance-result hypothesis give a complete picture of the investigation process. Thus, they are incapable of describing the effectiveness of detectives, in absolute terms or relative to patrol officers.

In direct contrast stands the *effort-result hypothesis*. According to this explanation, the investigative work of patrol officers and detectives contributes substantially to crime solution. Looking for witnesses, interviewing victims, checking records, cultivating informants, and other activities are efforts that increase the chances that an investigator may solve the crime. Initial leads spur investigative actions which can produce further leads and arrests. Though factors outside police control play a role, the effort-result hypothesis asserts that police actions substantially contribute to successful investigations.

Although it is supported more by public myth than by evidence, this hypothesis is also plausible and is not devoid of support from researchers. Both Ward (1971) and Folk (1971) suggest such a description in their studies. However, their research takes the effort-result hypothesis for granted, and they make no attempt to test its validity. In fact, until the late 1970s researchers had not tested the effort-result hypothesis. At most it had the support of common sense, but this was not scientific evidence. Even less support existed for this hypothesis than its rival.

In 1979, the Police Executive Research Forum began a study designed to describe how investigations are conducted (Eck, 1983). We used logs completed by patrol officers and detectives, official reports, and observations of investigators at work to describe the investigative process in three jurisdictions (DeKalb County, Georgia; St. Petersburg, Florida; and Wichita, Kansas). Investigators completed one log for each day a case was actually worked (a "case-day"). Our data describing actions taken by patrol officers and detectives investigating burglaries and robberies was shown earlier in Figures 2.1 through 2.5. We also documented the information produced by these actions, and the results of this investigative effort. Because we collected data on individual cases we acquired a detailed account of how patrol officers and detectives conduct burglary and robbery investigations from the preliminary investigation through an arrest or suspension of investigative effort.

With this set of data, we were able to avoid the three problems of earlier studies. We could control for the efforts of investigators and for case characteristics, and we could make comparisons between solved and unsolved cases. We could, therefore, test both the circumstance-result and effort-result hypotheses.

To test these two hypotheses, we analyzed only cases assigned to detectives for follow-up work. We used a multivariate procedure, logistic function analysis, suitable for a dependent variable with only two values (arrest and no arrest) to determine if detective effort increased the probability of arrests for burglaries and robberies. We controlled for information collected by patrol officers during the preliminary investigation. This allowed us to see if detective effort added to the chances of an arrest.

Detective effort was measured in two ways in two separate analyses.

First, we used the various actions taken by detectives—such as interviewing victims and witnesses, checking files, and interrogating informants and suspects—as effort measures. Second, we used information obtained by detectives—such as suspect name, suspect description, or link to another crime—to measure detectives' contributions.

If the circumstance-result hypothesis was correct, then information collected by patrol officers would be the only significant contributor to arrest. Neither the actions conducted by detectives nor the information they gained as a result of these actions would matter. If the effort-result hypothesis was correct, then the actions conducted by detectives and/or the information these actions produced would be significant contributors to arrests. Information collected by patrol officers would have little or no contribution to crime solution.

Table 2.1 shows the results of the analysis for the contribution of detective actions to the probability of arrest when we controlled for information from preliminary investigations. Four findings are immediately discernible:

> At least one piece of information from the preliminary investigation is significant in all three jurisdictions;

> Some activities of detectives are significant in each of the jurisdictions;

> Detective interviews of victims are not significant in any of the three agencies; and

> The importance of follow-up investigation activities (as measured by the number of significant activities) varies by jurisdiction.

The results are ambiguous. Preliminary investigation information is significant, thus supporting the circumstance-result hypothesis. Follow-up investigation actions are significant, thus supporting the effort-result hypothesis. Interestingly, Wichita, which organized its patrol officers and detectives into teams, had the greatest number of significant patrol activities. This result is consistent with previous research on the effects of increasing patrol involvement in investigations (Bloch & Bell, 1976). But even in this agency, detective activities were important for increasing the probability of arrests.

Table 2.1
Analysis of Follow-Up Investigation Activities
(Coefficients with Standard Errors in Parentheses)

	DeKalb Co.	St. Petersburg	Wichita
CONSTANT	-3.22(0.55)**	-2.40(0.69)**	-4.34(0.63)**

PRELIMINARY INVESTIGATION INFORMATION

	DeKalb Co.	St. Petersburg	Wichita
Witness	0.35(0.36)	1.38(0.95)**	0.99(0.53)
Suspect Information	-0.11(0.36)	-1.18(0.97)	1.27(0.42)**
Vehicle Description	-0.39(0.40)	-0.06(1.16)	1.43(0.51)**
Latent Prints	0.00(0.35)	0.18(0.62)	0.88(0.38)**
Related Offenses*	0.95(0.48)**		1.36(0.57)**
Range of Time of Occurrence	0.00(0.07)	0.20(0.12)**	0.03(0.13)

FOLLOW-UP INVESTIGATION ACTIVITIES

	DeKalb Co.	St. Petersburg	Wichita
Victim Interview	-0.71(0.49)	-1.27(0.67)	0.34(0.49)
Witness Interview	1.03(0.29)**	0.00(0.56)	0.86(0.48)**
Informant Interview*	1.37(0.35)**		
Other Interview	0.89(0.28)	0.50(0.60)	0.39(0.49)
Discussion with Dept. Member	1.08(0.30)**	1.02(0.50)**	-0.03(0.45)
Record & File Checks	0.81(0.29)**	1.23(0.51)**	0.64(0.42)**
Cases	849	212	597
R-square	19.8	8.9	13.5
Chi Square	132.48	18.10	52.47

* Insufficient data to test in all agencies.

** Significantly different from zero at .10 level of significance using a one-tailed t-test. A two-tailed t-test was used for the constant.

Follow-up investigator actions are a measure of investigative effort, but detectives conduct these actions to gain information. Therefore, we analyzed follow-up investigation information in the hopes that the results would be clearer. Table 2.2 shows the analysis results for the influence of follow-up investigation information on the probability of arrest controlling for preliminary investigation information. Two findings are evident:

> At least one piece of information from the preliminary investigation is significant in all three jurisdictions; and

> Suspect name and related crime information obtained by detectives is significant in all three jurisdictions.

Table 2.2

Analysis of Follow-Up Investigation Information
(Coefficients with Standard Errors in Parentheses)

	DeKalb Co.	St. Petersburg	Wichita
CONSTANT	-5.00(0.49)**	-3.66(0.66)**	-4.54(0.53)**

PRELIMINARY INVESTIGATION INFORMATION

	DeKalb Co.	St. Petersburg	Wichita
Witness	0.95(0.37)**	0.70(1.04)	-1.06(0.56)
Suspect Information	-0.54(0.36)	-0.91(1.06)	0.86(0.43)**
Vehicle Description	-0.43(0.45)	0.31(1.27)	1.66(0.54)**
Latent Prints	0.22(0.36)	0.50(0.73)	0.67(0.39)**
Related Offenses*	0.75(0.48)**		1.17(0.63)**
Range of Time of Occurrence	0.05(0.07)	0.40(0.15)**	0.05(0.13)

DETECTIVE FOLLOW-UP INFORMATION

	DeKalb Co.	St. Petersburg	Wichita
Suspect Name	2.82(0.44)**	2.24(0.69)**	1.60(0.42)**
Suspect Description	0.85(0.32)	-0.26(0.64)	-0.39(0.43)
Vehicle Description	0.42(0.34)	-0.17(0.76)	0.66(0.53)
Related Crimes	0.82(0.28)**	2.18(0.59)**	1.29(0.48)**
Cases	849	212	597
R-square	23.1	25.2	18.6
Chi Square	168.41	46.63	72.47

* Insufficient data to test in all agencies.

** Significantly different from zero at .10 level of significance using a one-tailed t-test. A two-tailed t-test was used for the constant.

Again the results are ambiguous. Maybe both hypotheses have some validity.

Although the data support both hypotheses, neither offers a complete description of the investigative process. Further, the two hypotheses are apparently contradictory. What is needed is a hypothesis that combines elements of both hypotheses and removes these contradictions. The *triage hypothesis* is such a hypothesis.

The triage hypothesis removes the contradiction by differentiating among types of cases. According to this hypothesis, the investigative process *implicitly* works to divide cases into three groups. These groups are:

1. Cases that *cannot be solved* with a reasonable amount of investigative effort;

2. Cases *solved by circumstances,* which only require that the suspects be arrested, booked, interrogated, and a prosecutable case prepared; and,

3.   Cases that *may be solved* if a reasonable level of investigative effort is applied to them, but will not be solved otherwise.

This is an implicit process because police agencies do not have policies (with one possible exception) to promote such a division. Instead, detectives, using their experience, create this division without setting out to do so. The one exception is case screening before cases are assigned to detectives.

The differences among these three groups are not as distinct as we have suggested. In fact, it may be more useful for us to think of these three groups as representing ranges of cases on a continuum. Still, the triage hypothesis makes it clear that we must differentiate between cases of the same crime type based on the level of investigative effort required to solve them. Group 1 cases require a great deal of effort, perhaps an infinite amount of effort, to solve. Group 2 cases required very little investigative effort to solve, though post-arrest processing efforts may be time-consuming. Group 3 cases fall into the middle range of investigative effort.

We can view the circumstance-result and effort-result hypotheses as special cases of the triage hypothesis. The circumstance-result hypothesis focuses on differences between group 1 and group 2 cases. The effort-result hypothesis focuses on differences between group 1 and group 3 cases.

The answer to the question, "Do detectives solve crimes?" is a qualified "yes." Detective work contributes to the solution of group 3 cases. But it does nothing for group 1 cases and little for group 2 cases. Circumstances beyond police control do have some influence and so do the efforts of investigators. In the three agencies we looked at, detectives made arrests in five to ten percent of the burglaries and robberies that did not have a named suspect when the cases were assigned to them. From 10 to 17 percent of the same cases resulted in detectives interviewing a suspect, even though they may not have arrested the suspect later. These are not large numbers but they are important. Though detectives may not be as omnipotent as the public myth (and some detectives) would have us believe, detectives are not as unproductive as earlier research had suggested.

IMPLICATIONS

The triage hypothesis allows us to draw distinctions among law enforcement agencies. Agencies with few resources, poorly trained, led, and motivated investigators, or having a low priority on investigations may implicitly assign more cases to group 1 at the expense of cases in group 3. For these agencies, group 2 cases will make up the majority of solved cases. Agencies with many investigative resources, well-trained, led, and motivated investigators, or with a high priority on investigations may do the opposite. In these agencies, cases that most other agencies would put in group 1, are implicitly assigned to group 3. So a greater proportion of solved cases may belong to this last group. Comparative agency studies are needed to determine how these organizational factors influence how investigators solve cases. This type of research would permit the development of performance measures for agencies and could lead to improvements in investigative effectiveness.

Differences in investigative strategies, tactics, and procedures may also influence the relative sizes of these groups. Agencies whose patrol officers conduct thorough preliminary investigations, have well-organized and accessible records, search for witnesses, and collect and process physical evidence may have a greater proportion of group 2 and group 3 cases than agencies that do not. Studies to assess the impact of these differences would be useful for confirming the triage hypothesis.

The question, "How many detectives are needed to effectively work a caseload of a given size," has received scant attention though such research can be valuable for making resource allocation decisions. Greenwood (1970) found no relationship between arrests and cases per detective for burglaries, but found a negative relationship for assaults. However, he did not distinguish between burglaries and assaults that detectives actually investigated (group 3 cases) and those that received only cursory treatment (group 1 and 2 cases). Thus, he overestimated the actual workload of detectives. Research on investigative caseloads should address the question, "What is the number of group 3 cases detectives can effectively work?"

Practitioners and researchers have usually been careful to distinguish among types of offenses (burglary, robbery, rape, homicide, larceny) but have paid little attention to differences in investigation difficulty. As suggested by the triage hypothesis, distinctions based on difficulty are critical for understanding how investigators work cases. Using offense types as a measure of case difficulty is meaningless because case difficulty can vary widely within these broad categories. Practitioners and researchers need to develop and refine investigative difficulty scales for use in performance measurement. Some early efforts have been made in this direction (Eck, 1983; Cohen & Chaiken, 1987).

The triage hypothesis opens up a number of management and research possibilities that could improve the functioning of investigations units. However, investigations seem to be a low payoff endeavor under even the best of circumstances. Therefore, it is unlikely that improvements in the way investigations are conducted or managed will have a dramatic affect on crime or criminal justice.

REFERENCES

Bloch, P. & J. Bell (1976). *Managing Criminal Investigations: The Rochester System.* Washington, DC: Police Foundation.

Bynum, T., G.W. Cordner & J.R. Greene (1982). "Victim and Offense Characteristics: Impact on Police Investigative Decision-Making." *Criminology,* 20:301-318.

Cohen, B. & J. Chaiken (1987). *Investigators Who Perform Well.* Washington, DC: National Institute of Justice.

Eck, J.E. (1979). *Managing Case Assignments: The Burglary Investigation Decision Model Replication.* Washington, DC: Police Executive Research Forum.

_____ (1983). *Solving Crimes: The Investigation of Burglary and Robbery.* Washington, DC: Police Executive Research Forum.

Folk, J.F. (1971). "Municipal Detective Systems—A Quantitative Approach." Technical Report Number 55. Operations Research Center. Massachusetts Institute of Technology.

Isaacs, H.H. (1967). "A Study of Communications, Crimes, and Arrests in a Metropolitan Police Department." In Institute for Defense Analysis, *Task Force Report: Science and Technology.* Report to the President's Commission on Law Enforcement and Administration of Justice, pp. 88-106. Washington, DC: U.S. Government Printing Office.

Gaines, L.K., B. Lewis & R. Swanagin (1983). "Case Screening in Criminal Investigations: A Case Study of Robbery." *Police Studies,* 6:22-29.

Greenberg, B., C.V. Elliott, L.P. Kraft & H.S. Procter (1975). *Felony Investigation Decision Model—An Analysis of Investigative Elements of Information.* Menlo Park, CA: Stanford Research Institute.

Greenberg, B., O.S. Yu & K. Lang (1973). *Enhancement of the Investigative Function, Volume I: Analysis and Conclusions.* Final Report, Phase I. Springfield, VA: National Technical Information Service.

Greenwood, P. (1970). *An Analysis of the Apprehension Activities of the New York City Police Department.* New York: Rand Institute.

_____ & J. Petersilia (1975). *The Criminal Investigation Process—Volume I: Summary and Policy Implications.* Santa Monica, CA: RAND Corporation.

_____ , J. Chaiken & J. Petersilia (1977). *The Investigation Process.* Lexington, MA: Lexington Books.

Police Executive Research Forum (1981). *Survey of Police Operations and Administrative Practices—1981.* Washington, DC: author.

Ward, R.H. (1971). *The Investigative Function: Criminal Investigation in the United States.* Ph.D. dissertation. Berkeley, CA: University of California.

3

Local Level Drug Enforcement*

David W. Hayeslip Jr.
National Institute of Justice

Deborah L. Weisel
Police Executive Research Forum

INTRODUCTION

Society's problem with the sale and use of illegal narcotics is an intergovernmental challenge that transcends any single public agency's ingenuity and resources. It is a problem which cuts a wide swathe through intergovernmental relations as a public health issue, involving the health care delivery system, public education, and the entire criminal justice system including law enforcement, the judiciary, and corrections. But the nexus of the drug problem is law enforcement simply because narcotics are illegal. Thus, the burden of responsibility for managing drug problems falls predominantly to local law enforcement agencies.

POLICE NARCOTICS ENFORCEMENT

Traditionally, enforcement efforts related to drug sales have been the responsibility of special narcotics units, organizationally housed within vice sections or divisions, in addition to the regular patrol divisions of local police departments (Moore, 1977; Williams et al., 1979; Manning, 1980; Skolnick, 1966, 1975).

---

* Opinions expressed in this chapter are those of the authors and are not necessarily those of the U.S. Department of Justice or the Police Executive Research Forum.

Officers assigned to narcotics units typically employed two basic enforcement strategies: "retrospective" and "prospective" (Moore, 1977: 129). Retrospective strategies were generally reserved for major narcotics distributors or wholesalers since police had to rely on their skills and persistence in reconstructing an offense based on standard police investigative techniques such as interviewing witnesses and examining physical evidence following the commission of a crime.

Prospective techniques, on the other hand, depended on the ability of the police to develop information leading to observations of illegal sale or use. Some techniques utilized under this strategy included direct observation of sales, development of search warrant cases, buy and bust techniques, and short- and long-term undercover operations (Moore, 1977:138-146). The use of informants has also been commonplace in prospective investigations.

The use of routine patrol as a tool in drug enforcement has been rather limited due to the difficulties in making drug arrests. Detection of drug violators was difficult for patrol officers because of the ease of drug concealment and even if drug deals were detected there are numerous constitutional constraints on searches and seizures (Moore, 1977:130). The success of patrol enforcement also depended on a number of factors beyond the direct control of the police, such as the willingness of members of the community to register complaints about drug dealing.

During the mid-1980s, however, the drug problem changed in America. Certain types of drugs, notably the rock cocaine known as crack, became widely available at a low price. The low price brought many more buyers and sellers into a new, highly competitive and volatile marketplace— American streets. For local police agencies, the new challenge created by widely available illegal narcotics was manifested in three different problems:

- Violence associated with highly competitive drug retailing spilled over into the community;

- Drug abuse was linked with other crimes that occurred in the community, especially street and property crimes; and

- The community's youth were attracted to the illicit markets.

These problems resulted in increasing public demands for a police solution. And because the nature of the drug market had changed so dramatically during this era, police tactics also were required to change. In particular, new tactics used to control wholesale distribution and retail sales and to reduce drug demand have been developed. In addition, some police departments are experiencing significant organizational change in response to these problems.

Wholesale Distribution

Police agencies have continued to focus on wholesale distribution networks, but this focus is now often through multi-jurisdictional task forces that combine the resources of federal agencies such as the Drug Enforcement Administration and sometimes Customs, Immigration, or the IRS; state police agencies; and local law enforcement agencies. A recent survey found that a large majority of police departments have joined forces in multi-jurisdictional task forces (IACP, 1988:78).

In addition, as drug wholesale networks have become more extensive and more impervious to criminal justice sanctions, law enforcement personnel have linked with prosecutors to put a new tool into effect: asset seizure and forfeiture. Federal laws, and in some cases state laws, permit law enforcement agencies to seize the assets of drug dealers and sometimes even drug purchasers. This has been thought to be a particularly effective tactic against dealers at the top of the drug distribution network who have often accumulated huge fortunes, including legal businesses, luxury automobiles and vast real estate holdings with their ill-gotten booty.

Retail Sales

Many more dealers emerged in the new drug markets of the late 1980s and sales were frequently conducted from heavily trafficked street corners that provided easy access to buyers. Sales were more often stranger-to-stranger and took place in "open air markets." Products—including price, quantity, and purity—became more homogeneous. The increased supply drove the price of the product down. A complicated network developed that consisted of a sentry, a bag man to hold the drugs, an actual drug seller and a nearby cache. Drug entrepreneuring, replete with business equipment such as cellular telephones and remote beepers, reached new heights in the poor neighborhoods where drug dealing was most common.

This changing retail market, along with mounting public concern, forced police to develop new and innovative policing strategies (Hayeslip, 1989). One of the most popular enforcement methods to combat drugs on the street has been the use of police saturation or police sweeps of troubled areas. The key difference between these saturation strategies and previous enforcement is that the need for personnel transcended the ability of the narcotics unit to staff the sweeps. Patrol officers have been widely used to conduct street sweeps. On occasions, these sweeps also feature "jump out" squads—groups of officers who swarm into a drug dealing location, arresting buyers and sellers. Other street sweep strategies have chased retail sales indoors to "crack houses" or "shooting galleries" where both sale and use of the drug take place. Indoor raids have been more difficult and time-consuming to execute, but are an important element of sweep strategies.

Police also have put asset forfeiture laws to use in their street-sales enforcement efforts. The law often allows for the civil seizure of assets used in the retail trade and officers have become more adept in their ability to invoke such laws. Other civil processes, such as abatement or nuisance property seizure, allow for the seizure of real property used in drug dealing. Many law enforcement agencies now routinely seize homes and cars. However, the use of asset forfeiture techniques at the retail level remains widely varied: its use is dependent upon the statutes of individual states, the cooperation of local prosecutors, the sophistication of law enforcement agencies, and the interest of police in building such cases.

During the era of changing law enforcement efforts against drugs, two philosophical policing strategies also have emerged as techniques for dealing with the drug problem and are being experimented with in a number of cities. One philosophy, community policing, relies upon the co-production of neighborhood safety as a joint effort between citizens and the police. Thus, typical community policing practices and programs include neighborhood watch groups, the use of foot patrols in troubled neighborhoods, positioning mini-stations in certain areas and establishing telephone hot lines to get citizen input and information on crime-related problems. The focus of most community policing programs is crime prevention. An important component of community policing is that the anonymity of motorized patrol policing is removed—officers get to know the people who live and work on their beats.

The other philosophical strategy of policing that emerged and was applied to drug problems was problem-oriented policing. This strategy does not advocate a ubiquitous solution to drug problems. Instead, the strategy involves carefully analyzing neighborhood drug problems, developing tailored responses to problems, and bringing together private and public resources, including the community, to solve problems. If poor lighting, or garbage, or truant youths contribute to the existence of a drug hot spot, then those conditions are viewed as contributing directly to the police problem. Thus, an officer might invest time to get the lighting improved, the abandoned vehicles towed, or even develop a recreational program to divert youths from hanging out on a drug corner. Police using this strategy are viewed as problem solvers who invest the time and resources necessary to effect a solution to a specific neighborhood problem.

Both community policing and problem-oriented policing rely heavily upon the efforts of uniformed officers to carry out the work. Unlike saturation techniques, neither community policing nor problem-oriented policing rely solely on invoking the criminal justice system as a response to a problem. These approaches do not eschew traditional methods but caution against automatic use of standardized responses as a panacea.

Demand Reduction

Although most contemporary police practices focus on the retail-supply side of the drug trade, police have increasingly adopted drug demand reduction efforts, that is, targeting the consumers of drugs. Traditional enforcement only occasionally addressed the user: police would arrest users for possession of illegal narcotics, usually incidental to another charge. Today, police are using many different law enforcement tools against drug consumers. For example, the police continue to arrest consumers for possession. However, these arrests are likely to be the result of reverse buy-bust operations orchestrated by the police. In these reverse stings, police pose as dealers and sell real drugs (or inert look-alike substances) to drug users. Once these deals are completed, other officers make the arrests.

Consumers also are targeted during street sweeps. As police saturate a drug dealing area, both buyers and sellers are arrested in an effort to disrupt the drug-dealing market. On some occasions, police also use civil forfeiture laws to seize the assets of consumers. For example, if an automobile was used to convey the buyer to the drug market, the car sometimes can be seized by local police because it is an asset used in the commission of a crime.

In an effort to further broaden the scope of consumer-oriented enforcement, some jurisdictions have sought and achieved statutory changes. For example, in some areas of the country, consumers can be arrested for public drug intoxication, driving under the influence of drugs other than alcohol, or loitering for the purpose of selling or buying drugs. These are other police instruments for reducing demand.

Organizational Change

Many police agencies have changed and adapted in order to respond to the changing drug market and public demands for a police solution to drug problems. Today, only rarely are drug enforcement efforts limited to narcotics and vice units. Although these units still retain primary responsibility for drug enforcement—especially wholesaling—other special enforcement units are also involved. Many local agencies have juvenile or gang units, violent traffickers' units, strike forces and other specialized units to deal with specific dimensions of the drug problem. But drug arrests in most jurisdictions are now more often than not made by uniformed officers.

On the philosophical front, neither community policing nor problem-oriented policing has achieved widespread acceptance in American police agencies. Although some agencies have adopted these strategies on a limited basis, programmatic implementation has been desultory. By far, retail-oriented sweep strategies predominate among the methods of policing used for drug problems. But there are substantial variances among law enforcement agencies in their drug enforcement efforts. Only as the problems within the nation's communities that are linked to drugs continue to escalate will thoughtful police administrators begin to get answers to the hard questions about the efficacy of the deployment of their limited human resources.

THE EFFECTIVENESS OF POLICE DRUG ENFORCEMENT

Historically, the primary goal of police drug enforcement has been to eradicate the business of illegal drug distribution by means of the criminal law (Williams et al., 1979). Theoretically, enforcement of the criminal law will control drug markets through general and specific deterrence, as well as incapacitation of those engaged in such activities. Criminal law sanctions have been thought to increase the costs and risks associated with drug sales, thereby reducing the benefits derived. By making the costs exceed the benefits, markets in illegal drugs will supposedly decline. Drug sales will no longer be profitable for dealers, so they will be forced to increase prices or stop dealing. As purchase prices increase and drug availability declines, established users will stop using drugs and recreational users and potential novices will no longer be attracted to drug abuse.

It also has been assumed that as the markets in illegal drugs are eradicated, crime will be reduced, particularly street-level and property crimes. It has been thought that drug users resort to crime in order to support their habits. By breaking the distribution chain the supply of illegal drugs will be cut off, user demand will cease and thus the crimes that would have been committed in order to secure money to buy drugs will not occur.

As described in the previous section, police departments have been structured and organized in ways thought to facilitate the achievement of these enforcement goals. Research has focused on the structures and processes of drug enforcement on the municipal level, and as Williams et al. (1979) have pointed out, a significant amount of literature has been written about "'ideal' practices." There are also numerous brief descriptions about how particular drug enforcement programs operate (see Crowley, 1986, for example). Unfortunately, however, very little is known about the effectiveness of drug enforcement efforts.

One of the earliest and best known examinations of police drug enforcement was Skolnick's *Justice Without Trial* (1966, 1975). The main focus of this work was on police use of discretion in the enforcement of particular laws, including vice and narcotics statutes. Skolnick found that because of the policeman's assigned task of maintaining public order and the substantial amount of discretion given to the police, a system of justice outside of the judiciary has been established. While this study is rich in its analysis of how supposedly professional police circumvent the letter and spirit of the law, its generalizability is limited since only one police department was studied in depth.

Williams et al. (1979), on the other hand, conducted case studies of drug enforcement units in six medium-sized cities across the country. Their study is primarily descriptive in nature in that it focused on the organization, budgets and operations of drug enforcement units. They presented a number of recommendations about drug enforcement ranging from personnel selection to necessary equipment. Their recommendations were primarily based upon qualitative data, however, since they found that sound evaluations of various enforcement strategies were difficult because of the levels of individual investigator discretion in determining specific enforcement strategies.

Moore (1977) analyzed the heroin distribution market and the police department's efforts to control it in New York City. During the course of his study a number of significant reforms were made in the Narcotics Division to increase efficiency and target higher level distributors (Moore, 1977: 197). Furthermore, the Patrol Division significantly increased its levels of arrests for narcotics violations. It appeared that as a result of these activities there was "an impressive attack on the lower levels of the distribution system," and that the Narcotics Division "succeeded in making cases against higher level violations" (Moore, 1977:191,197). He cautioned, however, that police arrest data should "be taken with a grain of salt" (Moore, 1977:191) since little was known about the actual numbers of users and sellers.

Indeed, as DeFleur (1975) points out, official police arrest data is poorly correlated with actual drug abuse behavior (DeFleur, 1975:99). She examined the activities and outputs of the Narcotics Division in Chicago and found that a variety of factors influenced the likelihood of arrest for narcotics violations. These included community pressures, changes in laws and policies and changing attitudes of the police toward minority populations (DeFleur, 1975:101), rather than the level of violations alone.

McDonald (1973) and Manning (1980) also examined how police organizations dealt with drug enforcement from an organizational point of view. They too present data concerning arrests and Manning also examined other indicators of efficiency, such as warrants. But as Manning concluded, these data are not very useful measures of the outcomes of drug enforcement efforts. One of the primary reasons measurement of enforcement effects was so difficult was that the police did not even know how many users there were. This problem was further compounded by the lack of data collected by police about the drug cases that they did pursue.

As Sherman (1990) has pointed out, police crackdowns became one of the most prevalent developments in policing during the 1980s, and recently, researchers have focused their efforts on evaluations of the effects of specific enforcement programs, most notably strategies which "crack down" on street-level distribution. One of the first of these recent evaluations was conducted in Lynn, Massachusetts. In Lynn, a vigorous enforcement strategy was implemented in order to disrupt an open and active heroin trade in the city. In this program, six state troopers and a detective from the Lynn Police Department were assigned to a drug task force whose primary purpose was to crack down on street sales by making such transactions difficult. Through undercover operations, surveillance and information from a drug hot line, arrests and the execution of search warrants increased substantially in the target area. The evaluation of this strategy suggested that its effects were quite dramatic. Heroin consumption appeared to decline, robberies and burglaries decreased and the visible street distribution disappeared with little evidence of displacement into substitute markets in the city (Kleiman, 1987).

In Lawrence, Massachusetts a program similar to the one implemented in Lynn did not appear to affect robbery and burglary, however. In addition, the availability of alternative street markets in neighboring areas appeared to draw purchasers away from Lawrence rather than forcing drug distribution to decline (Kleiman, 1988).

New York City also implemented a vigorous street-level enforcement program in Manhattan, known as "Operation Pressure Point." During phase one of this operation narcotics enforcement efforts were beefed up and a highly visible saturation patrol strategy was implemented (Bocklet, 1987). Arrests for narcotics violations, along with arrests for misdemeanors, increased significantly. Traffic and parking enforcement efforts in this area also were increased. The results of these efforts were similar to Lynn in terms of closing open markets and crime reduction although it was unclear whether or not market displacement occurred in the city (Kleiman, 1988; Zimmer, 1990).

In 1986 the Washington, D.C. Metropolitan Police began a citywide crackdown known as "Operation Clean Sweep" which relied on a large number of arrests at known drug markets. These efforts appeared to reduce the number of open drug markets slightly. However, drug abuse itself appeared to increase during the enforcement period as measured by urinalysis of suspects arrested and emergency room admissions (Reuter et al., 1988). In addition, as Sherman notes, drug-related violence escalated dramatically during this period (Sherman, 1989).

The Police Foundation recently examined the effectiveness of community-oriented and street-level enforcement efforts utilizing quasi-experimental designs in Oakland and Birmingham. This study's findings suggest that the treatments did affect property crime, citizen perceptions about drug trafficking, and citizen satisfaction with the police in Oakland. Similar effects were found in Birmingham and additionally a substantial decline in violent crime was noted (Uchida et al., 1990).

Thus, the evaluations which have been completed to date provide mixed and quite limited conclusions about the effectiveness of police drug enforcement. As noted above, on the one hand certain police drug enforcement strategies appear to have a favorable impact on crime and drug abuse, yet in other studies these impacts have not been identified as being likely outcomes of enforcement actions. Conclusions from these studies are complicated by methodological weaknesses and the difficulties in measuring the actual outcomes of police drug enforcement efforts.

FUTURE RESEARCH

While some promising evaluations of new and innovative police approaches to drug enforcement are underway, a whole range of issues must be addressed in the future before sound policy conclusions can be made about the utility of any of these approaches in combatting illegal drug distribution. In addition, studies of these issues should be methodologically more sophisticated than research which has been conducted in the past.

Issues

As noted previously, past research has pointed out that many police departments quite simply do not have a clear idea of what exactly is the nature of the drug problem in their jurisdictions. Many departments do not have an empirical picture of what types of drugs are being sold and used, where the markets are, and how the distribution network actually operates. Furthermore, some departments readily admit that they do not have the in-house analysis capability to develop baseline data on the nature of the drug problem, nor are they able to monitor changing trends in the nature of the problem in any scientific way. Of course, such baseline data is crucial to be able to examine the effects of any strategy which a department may choose to implement.

Along with information concerning the nature of the drug problem itself, more extensive research must be focused on the links between drug use, drug sales and crime. Such research should focus not only on the relationships between drugs and street and property crimes, but also should examine in greater detail how drugs and the increasing incidence of urban violence and homicide are related. The presumption has been that drugs are directly tied to such criminal activity, although there is significant confusion about what even constitutes a "drug-related crime."

Fundamentally, of course, future research on police drug enforcement must examine the effectiveness of various strategies. Any number of effectiveness research questions should be answered, such as: What impact do such programs have on drug abuse? To what degree are drug distribution networks disrupted, displaced or concealed by different types of programs? What are the deterrent effects on overall and specific drug use? What effects do various enforcement programs have on other elements of the criminal justice system? How are the public's attitudes concerning public safety and fear affected by various strategies?

Not only should such questions be addressed but future research should look at the effectiveness of drug enforcement efforts beyond the short term. Most previous work has examined effects within a relatively short time frame, yet long-term effectiveness, or lack of it, may be much more important.

Most police drug enforcement programs require a significant commitment of personnel, equipment and other resources. Future research should include examinations of the benefits (outcomes, not outputs) of these efforts compared to the costs associated with their operation. Furthermore, important questions need to be answered in terms of how police drug enforcement efforts compare to alternative approaches to reducing the supply of and demand for narcotics, including educational and other abuse-prevention efforts, interdiction, higher-level distribution investigations and traditional middle- and lower-level narcotics investigations.

Methodology

Most of these proposed research questions focus on the effectiveness of police drug enforcement programs. In order to answer these questions and others, more sophisticated research designs need to be implemented in the future.

Past studies, and most of the recent research, have either been primarily descriptive in nature or so narrowly focused on a single jurisdiction as to limit the generalizability of findings. In order to overcome these limitations, multi-site evaluations are warranted in the future. In addition, future efforts must go beyond descriptive analysis to examine in detail complex relationships in order to provide answers to the questions raised.

Ideally, more experimental evaluations which build upon those conducted in Oakland and Birmingham should be undertaken. In the absence of true or quasi-experimental approaches, at a minimum, well-executed pre-post strategy implementation evaluations should be developed. Furthermore, given that most previous work has looked at short-term effects, longitudinal designs should receive additional emphasis in the future.

IMPLICATIONS AND ISSUES

It is clear that little is actually known about what works in drug enforcement or how well it works. Certainly, the effectiveness of exclusively relying upon the criminal justice system by deploying more officers to make more arrests and seize more drugs has been called into question by a number of law enforcement executives. Thus, further research to determine the efficiency and effectiveness of current and alternative drug enforcement strategies is of vital importance.

But strategies of drug enforcement also must be crafted within the context of broader ethical and organizational issues that affect law enforcement agencies. For example, as Goldstein (1990) has pointed out, there is a growing recognition that solving the current drug problem will require more than just law enforcement; thus, effective drug enforcement efforts must be developed in concert with other public and private agencies. The effectiveness of such collaborative efforts must then be measured by more precise instruments than the traditional law enforcement measures of arrests, quantities of drugs seized, and value of assets forfeited. Instead, other measures, reflecting treatment for drug problems or the incidence of drug use among arrestees, for example, may be more appropriate.

Perhaps the most important drug enforcement issue requiring attention from the law enforcement profession is the troubling and recurring matter of police corruption, that is, the misuse of authority by police to secure material gain. Given the current drug markets, police corruption may become quite problematic, or as Carter and Stephens (1988:7) have concluded, "We must recognize that a tragic phenomenon is emerging in American policing with a new generation of police corruption associated with the drug trade."

Since a great deal of police work, especially in narcotics, occurs without written records or close supervision, corruption is a tangible threat to the efficacy of any drug enforcement effort. Corruption has historically occurred when laws are unenforceable, a problem that occurs when legislatures ban activities in which large numbers of people are engaged (Goldstein, 1977:197). Some may consider this descriptive of current drug use, and an echo of the nation's Prohibition era. However, as urban police agencies have responded to the drug problem by deploying greater numbers of officers for drug enforcement, more and more officers come into closer contact with those whom they are intended to control. Also, the use of informants and undercover operations brings officers into contact frequently with those whose illegal gains may be enticing.

Thus, many drug enforcement strategies may set police up to engage in certain kinds of corrupt activity such as failing to arrest violators, failing to adequately pursue leads which could result in arrests, failing to adequately inspect premises where illegal activities are known to occur, or appropriating drugs or money confiscated from users or dealers. More specifically, the various kinds of corruption common in law enforcement include the police taking bribes, using drugs, buying or selling drugs, taking confiscated property, conducting illegal searches and seizures, protecting informants, and using violence (Manning & Redlinger, 1986:50-56). The results of these kinds of corruption serve to severely impair the agency's credibility in enforcing drug laws, and undermine administrative control of the agency's officers (Goldstein, 1977:190).

The traditional responses to corruption—improved selection processes (including drug testing of recruits), improved training and increased levels and intensity of supervision—are hoped to give officers a clear sense of the outer limits of police abuse or supervision of their authority (Wilson & Kelling, 1982:35). Another procedure for preventing corruption is frequent and regular rotation of officers. This method is somewhat antithetical to progressive police efforts to bring police closer to the communities they serve, however. A balance must be developed between these competing objectives.

A number of ethical issues also are raised in drug enforcement. These issues range from decisions about where to focus enforcement efforts, to the implications of displacing drug-related crime into other areas, both of which raise questions about equitable distribution of police services.

Some strategies of drug enforcement also raise the specter of entrapment and pose a liability for police officers selling actual drugs; also, street sweeps sometimes sweep up people indiscriminately, and community policing and problem-oriented policing, by increasing police discretion, may increase the potential for police abuse of authority. These issues pale beside the larger corruption issue, yet are considerations which must be acknowledged when charting effective strategies for drug enforcement.

Perhaps a final global issue in which police drug enforcement strategies should be examined is determining realistic goals which the police can be expected to achieve. Common parlance in the early 1990s is to speak of the police as "solving the drug problem" or "fighting the war on drugs," idioms which imply a complete and final resolution to the nation's drug problems. The jargon contributes to the notion that the use of illegal narcotics in America, and concomitant drug-related crime, can be fully eradicated. Rather than perpetuating these myths, the criminal justice community may well wish to redefine goals in terms of managing community problems linked with drugs, such as reducing fear in elderly communities, or eliminating street sales in residential areas, or reducing property crime in business communities. If police are to be successful in developing and implementing effective drug enforcement strategies and achieving measurable results, a model must be developed that incorporates rational goals and reasonable objectives.

SUMMARY

If the police are to respond to the increasing community, political and media pressures to "do something" about drugs and violence in our cities, much more needs to be learned about what works best in drug enforcement, under what conditions and at what costs.

Future research also should examine the appropriate balance of police enforcement efforts with other public and private efforts to control illegal drug abuse. The ethical issues surrounding police drug enforcement efforts, such as the possibility of increased corruption, also must be studied in depth.

It will only be through such research that the police may make informed policy judgments about the implementation of drug enforcement program options in the future.

REFERENCES

Bocklet, R. (1987). "Operation Pressure Point." *Law and Order,* (February):48-52.

Carter, D. & D. Stephens (1988). *Drug Abuse by Police Officers.* Springfield, IL: Charles C Thomas.

Crowley, J. (1986). "A Community Puts a 'CAP' on Drug Pushers." *Law and Order,* (December):36-39.

DeFleur, L.B. (1975). "Biasing Influences on Drug Arrest Records: Implications for Deviance Research." *American Sociological Review,* 40,1:88-103.

Goldstein, H. (1977). *Policing a Free Society.* Cambridge, MA: Ballinger Publishing.

———— (1990). *Problem-Oriented Policing.* New York: McGraw-Hill.

Hayeslip, D. (1989). "Local Level Drug Enforcement: New Strategies." *NIJ Reports,* (March/April):2-7.

International Association of Chiefs of Police (1988). *Reducing Crime by Reducing Drug Abuse: A Manual for Police Chiefs and Sheriffs.* Gaithersburg, MD: author.

Kleiman, M. (1987). "Bringing Back Street-Level Heroin Enforcement." Summarized in *NIJ Reports,* 202(March/April):5.

———— (1988). "Crackdowns: The Effects of Intensive Enforcement on Retail Heroin Dealing." In M. Chaiken (ed.) *Street Level Drug Enforcement: Examining the Issues.* Washington, DC: National Institute of Justice.

Manning, P. (1980). *The Narcs' Game: Organizational and Informational Limits on Drug Law Enforcement.* Cambridge, MA: MIT Press.

———— & L. Redlinger (1986). "Invitational Edges of Corruption: Some Consequences of Narcotic Law Enforcement." In T. Barker & D.L. Carter (eds.) *Police Deviance.* Cincinnati, OH: Anderson Publishing Co.

McDonald, W.F. (1973). "Administratively Choosing the Drug Criminal: Police Discretion in the Enforcement of Drug Laws." *Journal of Drug Issues,* (Spring):123-134.

Moore, M.H. (1977). *Buy and Bust: The Effective Regulation of an Illicit Market in Heroin.* Lexington, MA: D.C. Heath.

Reuter, P., J. Haaga, P. Murphy & A. Praskac (1988). *Drug Use and Drug Programs in the Washington Metropolitan Area.* Santa Monica, CA: RAND Corporation.

Sherman, L. (1989). "Police Crackdowns: Initial and Residual Deterrence." In M. Tonry & N. Morris (eds.) *Crime and Justice,* Vol. 12. Chicago: University of Chicago Press.

———— (1990). "Police Crackdowns." *NIJ Reports,* (March/April):2-6.

Skolnick, J.H. (1966, 1975). *Justice Without Trial: Law Enforcement in Democratic Society.* New York: John Wiley and Sons.

Uchida, C., B. Forst & S. Annan (1990). "Modern Policing and the Control of Illegal Drugs: Testing New Strategies in Two American Cities." Unpublished draft final report to the National Institute of Justice.

Williams, J., L.J. Redlinger & P. Manning (1979). *Police Narcotics Control: Patterns and Strategies.* Washington, DC: Government Printing Office.

Wilson, J.Q. & G.L. Kelling (1982). "The Police and Neighborhood Safety: Broken Windows." *Atlantic Monthly,* 127(March):27-38.

Zimmer, L. (1990). "Proactive Policing Against Street-Level Drug Trafficking." *American Journal of Police,* 9,1:43-74.

4

Domestic Violence

Elizabeth A. Stanko
Brunel University

INTRODUCTION

Largely hidden from public view, violence in the home places women and children in much greater risk than any violence committed on the street. Violence in the home, so-called "domestic" violence, is by far the most prevalent form of violence confronting contemporary society. Its existence is not new. Only a small proportion of the violence is ever reported to any legal or policing authority. Feminist protest about the serious mistreatment of women and children by their patriarchal protectors has ripped open the closed front doors and has shown that most of the danger of women's and children's private lives come at the hands of husbands and fathers.

Traditionally, the police turned their back on violence in the home, unless, of course, they conducted a murder inquiry. (Lethal violence is typically committed by an assailant known to the victim, often the spouse or former spouse.) Police usually refused to be involved in what they characterized as "family quarrels." While there were of course exceptions in individual cases, there is no empirical evidence that shows that the police response to what they call domestic disputes was in any way helpful to women injured in the home.

The testimony of battered women underscored the frustration and terror suffered by women who sought police protection. In calling the police, women asked that the violence toward them stop. To do so, police have relied on four basic strategies: talking out the dispute among all parties; threatening all parties and then leaving; asking one of the parties to leave the premises to "cool off"; and (rarely) making an arrest (Parnas, 1972).

Police justifications for the rare use of the arrest option commonly revolved around their own assessments of women's seriousness about following through with criminal complaints and the appropriateness of police intervention into what they considered private "family" matters (Stanko, 1985). Feminist outrage about the danger of such responses culminated in civil suits against the New York City and Oakland police departments (Schechter, 1982; Gee, 1983). The success of a battered woman who sued the Torrington, Connecticut police department began to convince police departments that they could no longer financially afford to treat violence in the home differently from violence in the street (Woods, 1986).

Breaking the tradition of police nonintervention into violence in the home is the goal of current reforms taking place in a number of American police forces.[1] Inspired by the publicity surrounding the Minneapolis study (Sherman & Berk, 1985), police forces are adopting presumptive, and in some jurisdictions mandatory, arrest strategies in situations of misdemeanor domestic assault.[2] While police are assumed to arrest in cases of serious (felonious) assault, police reforms are meant to intervene into domestic violence before the violence grows too severe.

This chapter aims to address the following questions: What exactly do police do when they intervene into situations of violence in the home? Are the pro-arrest policies characteristic of recent research and are reform efforts really making women and children safer? Can women now be confident that police are aware of their need for protection? Will police alter their entrenched attitudes and behavior toward "private" violence through these reforms?

VIOLENCE IN THE HOME

To an outsider, policing violence in the home should be a simple matter. Typically, the victim already knows the name and address of the alleged assailant. Measuring the extent of the injuries need only be documented by a visit to the doctor. Crime solved. Unfortunately, it is rarely that straightforward.

To women or children terrorized in their own homes, violence may take many forms. Threats, verbal aggression, slaps, kicks, burns, punches or attacks with knives, guns or other weapons may constitute the violence on a particular day. Women who are battered report that they may know that the tension in the relationship is rising, signaling the danger of impending violence. Some women contact police during this stage and are told by the police to "call us back when he hits you." The actual form of the violence used by an assailant may depend entirely on the situation at a specific time. It may not be possible for a woman to reach for the phone and dial for help when violence erupts. Prior to the actual onset of violence, there is no need for police intervention.

The violence experienced by women and children in the home is not simply due to disagreements that may be resolved by the use of non-violent methods, but is often the result of the assailant's feeling that the woman somehow deserves to be punished or controlled. Batterers feel that they are entitled to make sure their wives and girlfriends act a certain way because they are the "men of the house." Some men who beat their children and female partners blame their aggression on drugs or alcohol (Kantor & Straus, 1987); others on frustration experienced from being employed or unemployed (Ptacek, 1988). Many women, despite suffering injuries, support their boyfriends or husbands during the "bad" times even though it may result in further harm. Women's socialization to be caring undermines their ability to label men's violence as criminal behavior (Stanko, 1985). Women, embarrassed by their failure to be good wives or girlfriends, rarely report any aggression they experience to friends and family, let alone to an authority such as the police. The structure of heterosexual relationships within a society founded upon gender inequality mitigates against women taking steps outside their own relationships to stop violence.

What happens within a particular relationship between a woman and a man is assumed to be the result of personality conflicts, different values, or personal quirks. Disagreements arise in most relationships, and fighting is assumed to be one of the ways of solving disagreements. If the violence escalates—which it typically does—the police are called when a particular beating gets "out of hand."

Enter the police. They may have been called by neighbors disturbed by the noise, by the frightened children or by the woman herself. Police, in responding to the call of a domestic disturbance, have no idea exactly what situation they may be encountering. But if the violence is reported in a private house and between parties who are living together or had lived together, the police often see the relationship or marriage as a very important part of the violence (Black, 1976).

How are the police to solve the problem of the particular call—a domestic dispute? Policing, after all, aims to "restore the peace" and if necessary arrest lawbreakers. But how is it possible for the police to restore peace in situations of private violence that are rooted in a particular history of heterosexual relations, constrained by societal expectations of coupledom, and informed by the specific interaction of an individual man and woman? And do they consider the actions of the assailant to be criminal actions?

SOLVING VIOLENCE IN THE HOME—THE POLICE ROLE

Police are the gatekeepers in the criminal justice system. Their actions dictate how and when a person is charged with a criminal offense, thereby subjecting that individual's behavior to the scrutiny of the court. For the officer on the street, an arrest is a welcomed break in the unpredictable routine of responding to queries, motoring offenses, and the usual calls for assistance in crimes such as burglary, shoplifting, or vandalism. Making an arrest, however, is not an everyday event.

Much of police work is geared to the resolution of conflict (Reiner, 1985). Blending the service element of police work with that of order maintenance, the officer on the beat acts as a 24-hour secret social service (Punch, 1979). Indeed, it is this part of policing that Bard (1970) fortified in the establishment of police crisis intervention teams to "sort out" the violence in the home. His approach was to train a team of police officers to act as crisis counselors in situations of acute family violence. This approach received a great deal of criticism from feminists who emphasized that what was needed in situations of acute violence is not counseling, but the arrest and removal of the assailant to prevent the occurrence of immediate and future violence.

Advocates for battered women demanded that the police not mediate men's violence in the home, but make arrests, charging the assailants with criminal offenses. The empirical evidence of the police response, however, concluded that police rarely arrest assailants (Parnas, 1972; Police Foundation, 1976). The findings of the United States Attorney General's Task Force on Family Violence call for the "legal response to family violence" ... to "be guided primarily by the nature of the abusive act, not the relationship between the victim and the abuser" (Hart et al., 1984:4). Violence in the home, the Task Force states, constitutes a crime and crimes are arrestable offenses. Is it as simple as that?

CHANGING POLICE RESPONSE: CAN POLICE DETER VIOLENCE IN THE HOME?

The clamor to reform the police stance toward violence in the home has led to a change in the ideological orientation of police chiefs and legislators. Throughout the 1980s, state legislatures in the United States passed legislation to enhance the police power to arrest batterers in the home (Ferraro, 1989a). Many states now require police to provide women with information on legal options such as obtaining orders of protection, to transport injured women to hospitals or to take women to shelters (Buzawa & Buzawa, 1985). Police therefore have a statutory obligation to see violence in the home as a criminal offense and to exercise the option to arrest the perpetrator(s) more often.

Encouraging, and in some jurisdictions requiring, police to arrest in situations of domestic violence attempts to prevent the escalation of violence. Theoretically, if the assailant is not punished for his abusive actions, then his behavior is tacitly condoned. An arrest would serve the purpose of labeling his actions as against the law and hopefully deter future violence. The belief in the deterrent effect of involvement in the criminal justice system is widespread in the prevention and prosecution of criminal matters. Researchers Sherman and Berk go so far as to conclude that arrest serves as an independent deterrent to future violence outside any additional effects of the court process (1984:270).

The Minneapolis experiment conducted by Sherman and Berk (1984) sought to empirically test the effect of different police responses to misdemeanor violence in the home. Participating officers were randomly assigned one of three response strategies: (1) arrest; (2) give some form of advice or attempt to mediate the matter; or (3) separate the disputants—the "walk around the block" solution. The researchers examined the effectiveness of these strategies in terms of how many offenders had at least one repeat incident of violence and how long after arrest the violence occurred. The results of the experiment prompted the researchers to conclude that police "should probably employ arrest in most cases of minor domestic violence" (Sherman & Berk, 1984:270).

The Minneapolis experiment captured the political spirit of the time. Police chiefs concerned by criticisms of their officers as well as worried about the possible financial burden of legal suits welcomed the experimental results. Preliminary findings of a national telephone survey of police forces in cities with populations of over 100,000 indicated that while 47 percent of city police forces still relied on the police officer's discretion in responding to a situation of violence in the home, 27 percent had adopted presumptive arrest policies (Sherman et al., 1985).

The rapid embrace of the pro-arrest message is based on the findings of but one research project. While the Minneapolis experiment is being duplicated in six United States jurisdictions (Garner, 1989),[3] questions are already being raised about the present practice of the Minneapolis Police Department and its own policy on domestic violence. Balos and Trotzky's (1988) examination of police response to domestic violence concluded that "despite statutes that would allow, and in some instances require arrest, and despite a stated Minneapolis police department policy of mandatory arrests, very few incidents of domestic violence resulted in arrests" (1988:94). Ferraro's (1989b) study of Phoenix, where a presumptive arrest policy exists, showed officers to be confused about what "presumptive" actually means and indicated that there was a wide gap between the ideological use of policy and its actual practice by officers on the beat.

Despite the publicity of the politically popular findings of the Minneapolis experiment, traditional police discretion determines the particular response in a situation of violence in the home. As always, discretionary decision-making, the bulwark of police power, remains in the hands of the rank-and-file officer who is far removed from the policy setting meetings attended by their supervisory officers. Examining the particular behavior of officers responding to violence in the home, researchers Berk and Loseke (1980-1981) suggest that police decisions about arrest are found in their interpretations of particular battering situations, their prior experience, and the situation-specific rationales for decisions inherent in the policing enterprise. These rationales "do not constitute an *abuse* of discretionary power, they are part of the *normal* exercise of duty" (1980-1981:343, emphasis in the original). Police, they found, seem to be affected by the demeanor of the assailant toward the police, the injury of the woman, the presence of witnesses, and the willingness of the woman to sign a criminal complaint. Worden and Pollitz (1984), whose research replicates and extends that of Berk and Loseke, suggest that officers differ in their orientations to the job, and these orientations affect how officers read the circumstances of violence in the home. The most important point here is that individual officers respond differently (Steinman, 1987). A victim of domestic violence, in distress and possibly injured, has no way of predicting whether the officer responding to a call for help will be of assistance.

As officer discretion continues to direct the police response in situations of violence in the home, individual officers may find themselves squeezed between a rock and a hard place. Stated one officer, "If you are really doing your job, you'll just get more complaints" (Stanko, 1989:63). Other officers may have never changed their traditional views about domestic violence as "just family quarrels" (Ferraro, 1989b). Another officer working in a state with statutory obligations concerning domestic violence remarked: "Come with me to a husband-wife fight. You arrest the husband and suddenly she's in love again" (Stanko, 1989:62).

What then might be additional impediments to the reform of police handling of violence in the home as criminal matters? Do we satisfy the demands of the public and feminists if we pass legislation and pressure police forces to take a more aggressive stance toward violence committed in the home? I fear not. We turn now to the internal organization of policing and to see how the internal workings of the rank and file might interfere with attempts to improve the policing of violence in the home.

OBSTACLES TO REFORM

I have suggested elsewhere (Stanko, 1989) that the occupational orientation of rank-and-file police officers provides important clues to how they might respond to situations of violence in the home. Images and expectations of masculinity, regardless of the gender of police officer, dominate the everyday context of policing (Hunt, 1984; Smith & Gray, 1983). Male attitudes about violence in the home reflect assumptions about what is understandable, if not proper, male behavior. Being aggressive, jealous, domineering or overcontrolling is associated with typical male behavior. Research examining the treatment of women's complaints of sexual assault by police officers has illustrated how this attitude translates into the everyday practice of minimizing women's reports about sexual violence (Randall & Rose, 1978). Although police have made strides in the handling of complaints of sexual assault, it is not unusual today for women to report they have encountered insensitive questioning at the hands of police.

In situations of violence in the home, it is most likely that a woman is the injured party. Even if police find that a man and woman admit to hitting each other, a woman is three times more likely to be injured in so-called "mutual combat" (Saunders, 1988). It is likely therefore that in assessing a situation of violence in the home a police officer scrutinizes the woman's behavior alongside that of her assailant, because both woman and man are assumed to have contributed to the onset of violence. When women are attacked by boyfriends, husbands, ex-husbands, or ex-lovers in their own homes, or by men known to them outside their homes—the most common forms of violence against women—it is difficult for police not to see the woman as somehow contributing to the occurrence and perpetuation of violence.

Handling violence in the home is not the sort of crime prevention police see as rewarding or even as "real" crime. Like the average citizen, police view real crime as "street" crime committed by strangers—usually young men against "innocent" citizens. Despite the rarity of "good pinches" (Van Maanen, 1978), police look forward to the day when they will encounter a crime in progress. This hope, suggests Van Maanen, helps "maintain the patrolmen's self image of performing a worthwhile, exciting and dangerous task" (1978:304). Those spending any time around rank-and-file police have heard the frustrating and cynical accounts of the many domestic disputes officers report. Although a few situations do involve personal rewards—saving the life or freeing a woman or child held hostage, most situations police respond to are events of violence that are entangled in the web of social, financial, and emotional dependence and are thus arduous, thankless tasks. They are the kinds of situations that do not lend themselves to "easy" solutions—or any resolution short of dissolution of the partnership and the willingness of the man, in most cases, to accept that the woman has decided to end the relationship.

Solving situations of domestic violence, police insist, should not be their job. Yet if legislation now requires police to act, and now specifies the type of action to be taken—the arrest of the assailant or providing access to information to the injured party—then whether they like it or not, police are legally bound to respond "appropriately." And, like it or not, police find that their competence as police officers—assessed by themselves and others to be that of maintaining public order—is now enmeshed in their ability to "sort out" the private order of an individual household. Whether it is fear of lawsuits or public criticism, police who ignore men's violence run the risk of being labeled negligent and incompetent.

POLICING VIOLENCE IN THE HOME: THE WAY FORWARD

Once within the conceptual framework of defining crime and criminal action, policing takes on the role of "solving" criminal matters. The decision to arrest is crucial in this context, for it functions as the first step in labeling behavior as criminal and morally unacceptable. While an arrest is only the first stage of criminal justice inquiry, it is the point at which crime enters the system. Ultimately, prosecutors make determinations about the criminal charge facing a particular assailant, and in situations of violence in the home, the criminal charges are likely to be reduced (Fagan, 1988).

Fagan (1988) suggests that criminal justice policy on battering has revolved around models of deterrence and sanction. These models rest upon explanations of individual action and seek to sanction and punish individual offenders for criminal behavior. Violence in the home, though, is much more complicated; the "bad apple" theory of violent aggression in the home focuses on the stresses and strains experienced by the individual offender. Feminist understanding of violence in the home, in contrast, links battering to power and domination. Men's violence, by far the most prevalent form of intra-household brutality, is legitimized and supported by institutional practice. Feminist intervention into violence in the home takes the needs of the woman, the most likely victim of intra-household crime, as the paramount issue. A feminist approach to the prevention of battering converges with a legalistic approach to punish the offender when the victim's life is at stake.

Regardless of the response of the whole criminal justice system, feminists and policymakers advocate the use of arrest as a strategy in the policing of violence in the home because not to use it has caused great pain and suffering. An oft-cited study showed that at 85 percent of the addresses where spousal homicides occurred, the police had visited at least once prior to the homicide, and in over half the homicides, the police had visited the homes at least five times (Police Foundation, 1976). If police had actually attended violence on so many occasions, why did they not *do* something? Additionally, women staffing shelters for battered women continue to hear numerous stories of police inaction from battered women. These stories have helped spur on legislative change and the creation of additional statutory obligations for police—an encouraging note to the many years of silence about woman abuse.

Police intervention is crucial in situations of acute violence in the family because such violence is life-threatening, endangering, and injuring. But police intervention will not alone magically transform any batterer into a loving, supportive husband. Nor will policing assist women in overcoming the innumerable obstacles presented by a society tied so strongly to gender inequality and heterosexual coupledom. In short, women are tied to men for many reasons—emotional, financial, societal—and as those working with battered women know, that tie is not easily broken in the worst of situations. That is why it is essential that the police join with feminists to create some safe space, and some safe time, for women to regroup and reconsider their options to live without violence. Police must become concerned about women as the targets of violence and facilitate, as much as possible, a woman's access to escape routes.

How do we convince police to intervene into violence in the home, given the occupational resistance of the rank and file to any tampering with their discretionary power? Are policy reforms, as Sykes (1985) suggests, merely creative illusions without the substance to change actual police practice? There is some evidence that the concerted efforts of some police officers can change the way violence in the home is treated. Female officers, according to Kennedy and Homant (1983), viewed violence in the home more seriously than their male colleagues. This suggests that hiring and retaining women in the force (Martin, 1989) is one mechanism for improving the lot of women battered in the home. If the police organization itself spotlights the handling and supervision of violence in the home as a priority, then we should expect promotions and recognitions to reward officers for their sensitive and decisive actions in situations of violence in the home.

Ultimately, cooperation with other agencies, especially ones promoting the economic independence and well-being of women, is the litmus test of police commitment to the issue of violence in the home. Police must reach out and forge bonds with shelters for battered women, child protective services, adolescent centers, welfare rights organizations, legal aid and housing advocates. Police can provide women with the link to others who might assist them. Police may be the ones outside a woman's immediate family who have witnessed the violence. Police organizations themselves should be realistic about what they can do, and support and reward officers who excel in empathy and sensitivity.

Police should be straightforward in their training of recruits about violence in the home, and should elevate training about violence in the home to the importance of any major crime. Ferraro (1989) and Balos and Trotzky (1988) starkly remind us that a change in policy without clear instruction to officers about how to implement the policy results in non-compliance. Any confusion is the responsibility of supervisory personnel who have not taken the time to explain and guide officers in their new duties. The resistance of officers to the policing of violence in the home should come as no surprise to any policymaker. Failure to recognize this resistance is inexcusable.

Nonetheless, the narrow focus on policing as *the* deterrent to battering is misguided and will lead to limited inroads in understanding, stopping, and preventing violence in the home. Policing violence in the home often means imposing a solution to violence tied to the criminal justice system. The victim, usually the woman, then loses control over how she is to stop the violence in her life. Women who drop criminal charges against their assailants may be using that action as one of the steps needed to negotiate safety. Women who follow through may decide that criminal justice intervention is essential to stop the pattern of abuse. Regardless of the course of action, however, women should have the autonomy and choice about what solution is best for them. This point of view is antithetical to how police exercise discretion in criminal matters.

CONCLUSION

Now, as police battle drug-selling gangs in the streets or frustratingly attempt to stay ahead of the creative minds of lawbreakers, the problem of violence in the home may continue to be relegated to the back burner. While police chiefs in our home towns are more often using the correct rhetoric about how violence is destroying the very fabric of our society—the family—their rank-and-file officers may carry on as usual. Ongoing studies and monitoring of police action in domestic situations are essential. Finally, though, we must be prepared to rethink the damage done by maintaining a society so deeply founded upon women's unequal status.

NOTES

1   Canada, Australia, England and Wales, and other countries have also undergone police reforms concerning the policing of domestic violence. See, for example, Hanmer, Radford, and Stanko (1989), Edwards (1989), and Bourlet (1990).

2   For a summary of legislatively mandated pro-arrest policies, see Ferraro (1989b).

3   The jurisdictions are Atlanta, GA; Charlotte, NC; Colorado Springs, CO; Dade County, FL; Milwaukee, WI; and Omaha, NE.

REFERENCES

Balos, B. & K. Trotzky (1988). "Enforcement of the Domestic Abuse Act in Minnesota: A Preliminary Study." *Law and Inequality,* 6:83-125.

Bard, M. (1970). *Training Police as Specialists in Crisis Intervention.* Washington, DC: U.S. Department of Justice.

Berk, S.F. & D. Loseke (1980-1981). "'Handling' Family Violence: Situational Determinants of Police Arrest in Domestic Disturbances." *Law and Society Review,* 15:317-346.

Black, D. (1976). *The Behavior of Law.* New York: Academic Press.

Bourlet, A. (1990). *Police Intervention in Marital Violence.* Philadelphia: Open University Press.

Buzawa, E. & C. Buzawa (1985). "Legislative Trends in the Criminal Justice Response to Domestic Violence." In A. Lincoln & M. Straus (eds.) *Crime and the Family.* Springfield, IL: Charles C Thomas.

Edwards, S. (1989). *Policing 'Domestic' Violence.* Beverly Hills, CA: Sage Publications.

Fagan, J. (1988). "Contributions of Family Violence Research to Criminal Justice Policy on Wife Assault: Paradigms of Science and Social Control." *Violence and Victims,* 3,3:159-186.

Ferraro, K. (1989a). "The Legal Response to Woman Battering in the United States." In J. Hanmer, J. Radford & E.A. Stanko (eds.) *Women, Policing and Male Violence: International Perspectives.* London: Routledge.

_____ (1989b). "Policing Woman Battering." *Social Problems,* 36,1(February):61-74.

Garner, J. (1989). "Replicating the Minneapolis Domestic Violence Experiment." Paper presented at the British Criminology Conference, July, Bristol, England.

Gee, P. (1983). "Ensuring Police Protection for Battered Women: The Scott v. Hart Suit." *Signs,* 8,3:554-567.

Hanmer, J., J. Radford & E.A. Stanko (1989). *Women, Policing and Male Violence: International Perspectives.* London: Routledge.

Hart, W., J. Ashcroft, A. Burgess, N. Flanagan, C. Meese, C. Milton, C. Narramore, R. Ortega & F. Seward (1984). *Attorney General's Task Force on Family Violence.* Washington, DC: U.S. Department of Justice.

Hunt, J. (1984). "The Development of Rapport Through the Negotiation of Gender in Fieldwork Among Police." *Human Organization,* 43,4:283-296.

Kantor, G.K. & M. Straus (1987). "The 'Drunken Bum' Theory of Wife Beating." *Social Problems,* 34,3 (June): 213-230.

Kennedy, D.B. & R.J. Homant (1983). "Attitudes of Abused Women Toward Male and Female Police Officers." *Criminal Justice and Behavior,* 10:391-405.

Martin, D. (1976). *Battered Wives.* San Francisco, CA: Glide.

Martin, S. (1989). *Women on the Move.* Washington, DC: Police Foundation.

Parnas, R. (1972). "The Police Response to the Domestic Disturbance." In L. Radnowitz & M.E. Wolfgang (eds.) *The Criminal in the Arms of the Law.* New York: Basic Books.

Police Foundation (1976). *Domestic Violence and the Police: Studies in Detroit and Kansas City.* Washington, DC: author.

Ptacek, J. (1988). "Why Do Men Batter Their Wives?" In K. Yllo & M. Bograd (eds.) *Feminist Perspectives on Wife Abuse.* Beverly Hills, CA: Sage Publications.

Punch, M. (1979). *Policing the Inner City.* London: Macmillan.

Randall, S.S. & V.M. Rose (1981). "Barriers to Becoming a 'Successful Rape Victim.' " In L. Bowker (ed.) *Women and Crime in America.* New York: Macmillan.

Reiner, R. (1985). *The Politics of the Police.* Brighton, England: Wheatsheaf Books.

Saunders, D. (1988). "Wife Abuse, Husband Abuse, or Mutual Combat?" In K. Yllo & M. Bograd (eds.) *Feminist Perspectives on Wife Abuse.* Beverly Hills, CA: Sage Publications.

Schechter, S. (1982). *Women and Male Violence.* Boston: South End Press.

Sherman, L. & R.A. Berk (1984). "The Specific Deterrent Effects of Arrest for Domestic Assault." *American Sociological Review,* 49:261-272.

Sherman, L., J. Garner, E. Cohn & E. Hamilton (1985). "The Impact of Research on Police Practices: A Case Study of the Minneapolis Domestic Violence Experiment." In S.E. Hatty (ed.) *National Conference on Domestic Violence Proceedings.* Canberra, Australia: Australian Institute of Criminology.

Smith, D.J. & J. Gray (1983). *Police and People in London.* London: Policy Studies Institute.

Stanko, E.A. (1985). *Intimate Intrusions.* London: Routledge.

———— (1989). "Missing the Mark? Policing Battering." In J. Hanmer, J. Radford & E.A. Stanko (eds.) *Women, Policing and Male Violence: International Perspectives.* London: Routledge.

Steinman, M. (1987). "Arrest Policies and Spouse Abuse: Putting a New Policy Direction in Perspective." *American Journal of Police,* (Fall):11-25.

Sykes, G.W. (1985). "The Functional Nature of Police Reform: The 'Myth' of Controlling the Police." *Justice Quarterly,* 2(March):52-65.

Van Maanen, J. (1978). "Observations on the Making of Policemen." In P. Manning & J. Van Maanen (eds.) *Policing: A View from the Street.* Santa Monica, CA: Goodyear.

Woods, L. (1986). "Resource List: Battered Women Litigation." New York: National Center on Women and Family Law.

Worden, R.E. & A.A. Pollitz (1984). "Police Arrests in Domestic Disturbances: A Further Look." *Law and Society Review,* 18,1:16-34.

5

Crime Prevention

Knowlton W. Johnson
University of Louisville

Stephen L. Merker
University of Louisville

INTRODUCTION

Crime and fear of crime are well-known threats to the quality of life in urban and rural communities of our nation (American Psychological Association, 1984; Brown, 1984; Skogan, 1986; U.S. Department of Justice, 1983). Among victims of crime, fear is one of the most common and lasting reactions from the experience. The process of coping with victimization has been described as one of rebuilding the assumptive world with the belief in "personal invulnerability" as one of the most critical assumptions affected by victimization (Janoff-Bulman & Frieze, 1983). Recent studies have found evidence that victims of more severe crimes remain more fearful than victims of less severe crimes for at least four months following the incident, although the more general trend is for effects of victimization on psychological distress to cease by the end of four months (e.g., Cook, Smith & Harrell, 1987). It also has been found that victims within the general population have more fear than nonvictims for considerably more than a year after the incident, although the depressive symptoms present in the first few months dissipate over time (Johnson, Norris & Burgess, 1986).

In recent years there has been a noticeable public policy shift from concern about offender rehabilitation and defendants' rights to concern about victims. In the 1970s and 1980s, the Department of Justice supported a number of crime victim initiatives having implications for the entire nation (Bureau of Justice Statistics, 1986; President's Task Force, 1982). Additionally, some 40 states have enacted victim compensation programs, and 17 states have enacted victim Bills of Rights (Bard & Sangrey, 1986). The victims' movement has burgeoned into a major social force, stimulating the development of programs and legislation affecting victims and potential victims of crime.

In regard to law enforcement initiatives concerning the victims of crime, state and local officials have elected not so much to sponsor programs targeted specifically for crime victims but rather to initiate crime prevention programs that focus on the general population, which includes victims and potential victims of crime. (These programs are discussed later.) Perhaps of all the initiatives launched as solutions to the threats of crime and the fear of crime, more police departments across the nation have promoted "self-help" prevention measures among citizens than any other crime prevention strategy. Many crime prevention programs, as one facet of their total effort, encourage citizens to take deliberate precautionary measures such as installing deadbolt locks and alarm systems, marking property, checking for identification, or making sure their automobiles are locked at all times when not occupied. The assumption is that these types of actions will prevent victimization and will reduce the level of fear of being victimized.

Recently there has been research that questions this crime prevention strategy. In 1987, the Kentucky Criminal Justice Statistical Analysis Center (SAC) released the results of a statewide longitudinal study that found "self-help" measures initiated by citizens, e.g., installing burglar alarms and taking other individual precautions, to be insufficient in reducing the actual chances of citizens being victimized or in reducing fear of the victimization experience (Norris & Johnson, 1987). This study stimulated an international discussion about law enforcement's promotion of self-help measures as an effective crime prevention initiative (e.g., "Crime Prevention Measures," 1987; International Association of Chiefs of Police, 1987; Miller, 1988). In 1988, an article appeared in the *Journal of Urban Affairs* which continued the discussion in academic circles (Norris & Johnson, 1988).

The study presented here is, in part, a replication of the 1987 Kentucky SAC study which addressed the efficacy of only one of the many law enforcement initiatives launched as solutions to the threats of crime and fear of crime: the promotion of "self-help" prevention measures among citizens. The study examines the effects of various self-help measures on fear and subsequent victimization experienced by crime victims, not only when initiated independently, but also when initiated in collaboration with formal crime prevention programs.

CRIME PREVENTION STRATEGIES:
A REVIEW OF THE LITERATURE

Concern over crime and the fear of crime has prompted the development of diverse programs and strategies in our nation. As stated earlier, these crime prevention strategies have not primarily singled out victims as a special target population but have treated them as part of the general population.

The effects of innovative police practices, environmental design, citizen participation, and citizen-initiated preventive measures appear to have been studied most often. The results of attempts to reduce crime or fear of it through innovative police practices have been mixed. In a Kansas City experiment, preventive patrols designed to increase the visibility of the police had no effect on either the actual amount of crime or on the fear of crime. However, in another study, foot patrols were found to reduce the fear of crime. The COPE (Citizen-Oriented Police Enforcement) project found "directed" patrol to be of little value for reducing fear of crime, but contacts between the police and citizens aimed at solving specific neighborhood problems showed considerable promise. Experiments in Houston, Texas, and Newark, New Jersey found that an aggressive program of expanded contacts between police and citizens can reduce overall fear of crime (Cordner, 1986; Kelling, Pate, Dieckman & Brown, 1974; Pate, Wycoff, Skogan & Sherman, 1986; Police Foundation, 1981).

There also have been mixed findings on the effects of neighborhood watch programs which are known mostly for promoting citizen involvement in protecting their own communities. Although there have been numerous evaluations of neighborhood watch programs that have reported reductions in crime, and occasionally, reductions in fear of crime, nearly all of the program evaluations were seriously flawed. Of the two programs that have been rigorously evaluated, the well-known Seattle evaluation yielded positive results, showing a reduction in residential burglary in the target areas relative to the control areas. In contrast to the Seattle evaluation, another team found evidence in their evaluation of a Chicago neighborhood watch program of an increase in a variety of social problems, including fear of crime and vicarious victimization (Cirel, Evans, McGillis & Whitcomb, 1977; Lindsay & McGillis, 1986; Lurigio & Rosenbaum, 1986).

"Crime prevention through environmental design" and "defensible space" designate yet another set of strategies promoted as effective approaches in reducing crime and fear. These programs seek to reduce opportunities for actual crime and thereby reduce fear by restructuring the urban environment. Poor lighting, blind spots, and pedestrian traffic patterns are examples of physical attributes of the environment that may combine to produce a high risk of victimization and high level of fear. While there have been few evaluations of environmental design programs, Oscar Newman's well-known research of the early 1970s concerning defensible space strongly suggested that crime in public housing could be reduced by introducing physical changes in the dwellings. In the early 1980s, an evaluation of the Hartford project examined the effects of a number of physical changes that were implemented along with other changes in policing the neighborhood and in involving citizens in neighborhood activities. The findings were somewhat less than conclusive. The results showed some overall reductions in the levels of crime and fear, but no effects could be attributed directly to the program, particularly to its efforts to redesign the environment (Fowler & Mangione, 1982; Henig & Maxfield, 1978; Jeffery, 1971; Newman, 1972).

Of all crime prevention strategies, promoting citizen-initiated precautions or "self-help" measures has been one of the most commonly used law enforcement responses. Its popularity stems, in part, from proponents' claims that reductions in the probability of being victimized and in the level of fear are both viable results. Moreover, self-help measures are inexpensive to implement. Possibly as a result of widespread promotion, self-help measures are commonly used in American households. Nationally, it has been reported that one in four adults has had valuables engraved. Statewide surveys report that a large majority of citizens take self-help measures such as leaving their lights, radios, or televisions on when away from home and asking for identification from service and delivery personnel (Duncan, 1980; Johnson & Hardyman, 1987; Johnson et al., 1986; Lavrakas, 1985; Whitaker, 1986).

Like other crime prevention strategies, the effectiveness of campaigns that promote self-help measures is far from conclusive because these measures usually have been implemented along with other preventive measures. In an evaluation of a Monterey County, California program of burglary prevention that heavily emphasized self-help measures, a time series analysis showed that the program failed to affect crime rates. Further, the previously mentioned Kentucky SAC study found self-help precaution behavior insufficient to prevent crime or to reduce the fear of crime. In contrast, evaluations of programs in Seattle and Minneapolis, where self-help measures were promoted along with other strategies, showed that such programs can produce reductions in crime and/or the fear of crime (Cirel et al., 1977; Johnson, 1980; Kaplan, Palkovitz & Pesce, 1978).

METHODS AND PROCEDURES

Sampling and Data Collection

This study is a secondary analysis of data collected as part of the Kentucky SAC crime estimation program (Johnson & Hardyman, 1987). The sample for this study consists of 376 respondents, generally representative of adults in Kentucky, who participated in both interviews of a two-wave longitudinal study conducted from July 1986 to June 1987. The first wave of data reflects crime incidents, fear of crime, and use of precaution measures reported between January and December, 1986; the second wave of data reflects crime incidents, level of fear, and use of precautionary measures reported between July, 1986 and June, 1987.

Initially, 460 households were randomly selected using random digit dialing (RDD) procedures to assure that every household with a telephone had an equal probability of inclusion in the sample (Waksberg, 1978). (Approximately 88% of Kentucky households have telephones.) Within each household selected to complete the interview, one person was selected randomly from all adult members (age 18 or older) of the household. He or she was asked to report incidents of criminal victimization for all persons residing in that household. The length of the interview was, on an average, 10.8 minutes for nonvictims and 13.2 minutes for victims.

At the outset of data collection, the sample was divided into six equal groups. The first group was contacted in July and asked to report incidents of crime that occurred between January and June of 1986. The second group was contacted in August and asked about crimes that had occurred between February and July of 1986. In September, the third group was contacted and asked about crimes occurring between March and August 1986. This process was repeated until each of the six sample groups had been contacted and questioned twice about crime incidents occurring in the previous six months. This system, patterned after the one used by the Bureau of Justice Statistics for the National Crime Survey (NCS), controlled for the effects of forgetting by focusing on a recent, bounded period of time (U.S. Department of Justice, 1986).

From the original group of households that were contacted (747), 460 respondents completed the first interview, representing a response rate of 62 percent. (There were only 1% terminations and 15% refusals. Other reasons for not responding to the interview included no answer, moved, and died.) A total of 376 respondents also completed the second interview six months later, representing 82 percent of the original group.

Data were compared with the projected 1986 demographic characteristics of Kentucky residents as compiled by the University of Louisville's

State Data Center (Urban Studies Center, 1986). These comparisons found that the percentages obtained for race were comparable to those in the census data (i.e., sample 95% white, 5% non-white; and population 92% white, 8% non-white). However, there appeared to be an oversampling of females and persons over 30 years of age. (This gender imbalance between the sample and the general population was adjusted through poststratified weighting procedures when making statewide crime comparisons in the larger project; for this secondary analysis, which focuses on precautionary behavioral effects among victims, gender and age were entered as a statistical control in all analyses.)

Comparisons of selected background characteristics between the 376 households in which a member of the household responded to the Wave 1 and Wave 2 interviews and those 84 households that did not participate in the Wave 2 interview revealed only one statistically significant difference. Gender of the household respondent significantly differed across the two groups; more female respondents participated in both interviews than male respondents. Other characteristics of the household—residence (urban or rural), number of household members, number of children in the household, characteristics of the household respondent, education, age, and employment status of the household respondent—were not significantly different between the two groups.

Most of the 376 respondents were white (95%) females (74%), of whom a little over half (59%) lived in an urban area of the Commonwealth. Fewer than half of the respondents were full-time or part-time employees or students (43%); the remaining 57 percent were disabled, retired, or housewives. The ages of the respondents ranged between 18 and 94 years with the average age being 45 years old. The level of educational achievement reported by the respondents indicated that most did not have a college education; 17 percent had less than nine years of formal schooling, and 54 percent had between nine and 12 years of schooling. A quarter of the respondents had attended college or business school with 5 percent attending graduate school. The number of household members ranged from one to eight and the number of children in the household ranged from zero to six.

Measures

Victimization

Victimization was measured in both waves by a battery of questions modeled after those used in the National Crime Survey (Lehnen & Skogan, 1981). Respondents were asked to report the experiences of all members of their household, including their own, over the previous six months. A series of 20 "screener" questions was first asked to determine whether the household had been exposed to any crime or other potentially illegal event. The screener questions were followed by detailed questions designed to reveal the specifics of each of the incidents reported. Each respondent was asked about specific recent experiences (actual and attempted incidents) of crime in a variety of categories. Questions tapped personal victimization (i.e., robbery, rape, murder, actual assault, and purse snatching) and property victimization (burglary, theft, vandalism, and auto theft).

Of the 376 households included in the longitudinal study being reported, 19.9 percent were victimized in the first six months and 9.6 percent of the households contained crime victims during the second six months. Some households reported a crime in both waves of data. The above-average rate of crime for the first half of 1986 is almost certainly the result of telescoping, i.e., reporting crimes beyond the specified six-month period—when first interviewed, respondents had to accurately remember the previous six months without the aid of a dramatic milestone as their starting point, whereas the second interview could focus more concretely on the time period since the first interview. While this common problem can affect crime estimating, which was the purpose of the larger project, it is not a problem in an analysis of the effect of precautionary behavior and victimization on the fear of crime using two waves of data.

Fear of Crime

Fear of crime was assessed by asking household respondents a series of six questions related to worrying about being a victim of crime and to feeling safe in one's environment. These items were found to form a valid and reliable scale in previous studies of Kentucky (e.g., Johnson & Norris, 1986). The six items, each of which has a four-point response format, are as follows:

1. "How safe do you feel walking alone in your neighborhood during the day?"

2. "How safe do you feel outside in your neighborhood at night?"

3. "How much does the fear of crime prevent you from doing things you would like to do?"

4. "When you leave your house or apartment, how often do you think about being robbed or physically assaulted?"

5. "When you leave your house or apartment, how often do you think about it being broken into or vandalized while you're away?"

6. "When you're in your home, how often do you feel afraid of being attacked or assaulted by someone that you know such as a relative, neighbor, or acquaintance?"

A factor analysis of both Wave 1 and Wave 2 data supported the unidimensionality of the scale with factor loadings exceeding 0.50. The scale has moderate-high internal consistency at both waves (Wave 1 alpha = .76; Wave 2 alpha = .78). The stability of this measure over six months (i.e., test-retest reliability) was also moderate-high (r = .78). The scale was scored so that the higher the score, the higher the fear. Scores ranged from 6 to 24 with means of 11.9 and 11.5 at Waves 1 and 2, respectively.

Crime Prevention Measures

Two sets of crime prevention measures were used in this study—behavior that can be initiated independently by individual citizens (self-help measures) and behavior taken under the guise of state and local government crime prevention programs (program participation measures). Ten self-help precautionary measures were included in the study. Coded 0 (no) or 1 (yes), the items were: use dead-bolt locks; lock doors and windows when away; lock vehicles at home and when away from home; have valuables engraved; use antiburglary stickers and decals; ask service personnel for identification; have burglar alarm; leave lights, radio, or television set on when away; have a neighbor keep an eye on things while away; and have friends pick up the mail when away. Skogan and Maxfield (1981) refer to these measures as household protection behaviors.

Residents also were asked if they participated in neighborhood watch programs or if neighbors informally watched one another's homes and property. Participation in Operation Identification was assessed by noting how many citizens obtained antiburglary decals and/or had their valuables engraved through this program.

Factor analyses revealed that the self-help measures were relatively independent of each other; an exception to this pattern was the use of decals and engraving property (r = .47) which are measures administered through Operation Identification programs implemented in the state. Other correlations ranged from .24 to -.01 with most correlations being below .10. Low participation in two of the three crime prevention programs restricted the use of factor analyses on the variables. Even though we found only two self-help measures that factored together, i.e., use of decals and engraving property, the assumption was made that the ten self-help measures represent conceptually a general precautionary behavioral orientation regardless of the lack of empirical interrelatedness of the measures. Further, it was assumed that this general behavioral orientation of precaution would be more effective in reducing the fear of crime than use of any specific self-help measure or participation in a particular program. Therefore, indices which measure the scope of precautionary behavior without regard to the particular types of behaviors may correlate with varying levels of fear.

Two indices were constructed by summing the "yes" responses to the ten precaution items (range = 0-10) and the responses to participation in the three formal programs (range = 0-3). The mean score was 5.3 on the precaution index and .34 for the program participation index. Only content validity was established, however, the test-retest reliability was high, both for the precaution index ($r=.84$), and for the program participation index ($r=.85$).

Vulnerability Measures

Seven vulnerability measures were included in the study because previous research has suggested that they are related to the fear of crime, victimization, or both. Three were personal characteristics: age (in years), sex (female = 0; male = 1), and education (in years). Two measures described the composition of the household: number of adults and number of children. The final two measures were included as measures of "lifestyle": residence (rural = 0; urban = 1) and employment activity (homemaker, retired, or disabled = 0; worker or student = 1).

RESULTS

Crime Victims and their Involvement in Crime Prevention

Table 5.1 presents a comparison of crime victims' and nonvictims' use of crime precaution measures and participation in crime prevention programs. Asking a friend/neighbor to keep an eye on one's home while away is the self-help measure most frequently practiced by Kentucky residents. Nearly nine out of ten (89%) of Kentucky residents reported asking someone to keep an eye on their home while they were away. Other measures frequently reported were asking a friend/neighbor to pick up the mail (82%) and leaving the lights, radio, or TV on when away at night (74%). Locking the doors and deadbolting the doors of their homes and locking car doors were also common tactics practiced by Kentucky residents (68%, 56%, and 58%, respectively). It appeared that very few homes (7%) had burglary alarms.

Significant differences in the use of precaution measures of victims and nonvictims were found for only two precaution measures. As shown in Table 5.1, 80 percent of the crime victims use locks on doors at home and 70 percent lock their car doors as compared to only 65 percent and 55 percent of the nonvictims, respectively. More victims also engrave valuables (57%) than nonvictims (35%).

Table 5.1
Use of Self-Help Precaution Measures
Among Crime Victims and Nonvictims in Kentucky

Utilization of Self-Help Measures	Victim %	Nonvictim %	Total N	%
Ask friend/neighbor to keep eye on home	92	88	334	89
Ask neighbor/friend to pick up mail	84	81	308	82
Leave lights, radio, or TV on at night	81	72	275	74
Use locks on doors of home*	80	65	256	68
Use deadbolts on doors of home	66	54	211	56
Use locks on doors of car*	70	55	202	58
Engrave valuables**	57	35	148	40
Ask repair person for identification	47	44	166	44
Have antiburglary stickers on windows	25	15	65	17
Have burglar alarm	10	6	24	7
Participation in Formal Programs				
Engrave valuables/anti-burglary stickers through Operation Identification	28	19	78	21
Participation in police-sponsored Neighborhood Block Watch	6	5	16	5
Sought advice from crime prevention specialists	4	2	9	2

* Significant difference between victims and nonvictims at p < .05

** Significant difference between victims and nonvictims at p < .01

Overall participation in formal crime prevention programs by Kentucky residents was low. The program in which the largest percentage of residents participated was Operation Identification; 21 percent reported engraving their valuables or obtaining antiburglary stickers through the Operation Identification program. Very few participated in police-sponsored block watches (5%) or sought advice from crime prevention specialists (2%). Crime victims and nonvictims did not vary significantly on their participation in formal crime prevention programs.

Precaution as a Fear-Reducing Strategy

Our assumption was that "self-help" crime precautionary measures would be more effective in reducing fear among crime victims than among nonvictims. We further assumed that participation in formal crime prevention programs would produce even greater effects among victims than nonvictims. (It is important to restate that this study focuses on citizens whose households were victimized within a 12-month period; nonvictims are those citizens whose households did not experience an incident of crime during that period.) These results are presented in Tables 5.2 and 5.3.

Effects of Individual Crime Prevention Activities

In Table 5.2, results are presented which display the relationships between each of the 10 self-help measures and fear of crime. Participation in only one of the three crime prevention programs under study (Operation Identification) could be considered in the analysis because so few respondents reported being involved in formal programs. We also used multiple regression as the statistical technique which controls for the effects of other variables when analyzing an effect of a particular self-help measure. The bivariate correlations and the betas that appear in the final equation are reported in each table.

Controlling for vulnerability factors—age,[1] education, gender, employment status, residence (rural, urban), number of adults, and number of children—and victimization at Wave 1, only one of ten self-help measures significantly correlated with fear. This significant effect concerned respondents who reported that they generally lock doors when away; they also reported that their fear was higher than those respondents who did not practice this self-help measure (Beta = .15, p < .01). The effects of leaving lights, radio, or TV on when away and locking car doors were almost statistically significant. Participation in Operation Identification had no significant effect on respondents' levels of fear at Wave 1.

Table 5.2
The Effects of Self-Help Measures, Operation Identification Program,
and Victimization on Fear and the Persistence of Fear:
Results from a Multiple Regression Analysis

Variable(s) Entered	Fear (Wave 1)		Fear (Wave 2)	
	r	beta	r	beta
Fear W1	NA	NA	.78***	.73***
Vulnerability Measures				
Age	-.02	-.06	-.01	.03
Education	-.22***	-.25***	-.20***	-.05
Residence	.08	.04	.12*	.02
Gender	-.21***	-.17**-	-.22***	-.05
Number of adults	.05	.05	.07	.11
Number of children	.02	-.04	.00	-.11*
Employment status	-.08	-.00	-.06	-.02
Self-Help Measures				
Deadbolt on door	.07	.00	.11*	.07
Lock doors of home	.24***	.15**	.20***	.08
Lock car	.19***	.11	.08	-.10*
Engrave valuables	.03	.02	.02	.00
Decals on windows	.07	.03	.05	.00
Leave lights, radio, or TV on at night	.11*	.11	.15**	.06
Ask neighbor to keep eye on home	.07	.03	.06	-.03
Ask neighbor to pick up mail	.07	.03	.06	.01
Have burglar alarm	.04	.04	.03	-.01
Ask repair person for I.D.	.13**	.02	.17**	.06
Operation Identification				
Program	.02	.05	-.01	.03
Victimization Measures				
Victimization W1	.21***	.17**	.20***	.04
Victimization W2	NA	NA	.23***	.08*
R^2		.21		.65
(df)		(19,300)		(21,298)

Notes: * $p < .05$
        ** $p < .01$
        *** $p < .001$

In Table 5.2, results are also reported that show the relationship between particular crime prevention measures and persistence of fear of crime (Wave 2 fear controlling for Wave 1 fear) being somewhat different than at Wave 1. Respondents' locking their car was the only self-help measure which significantly correlated with the level of fear six months later (Beta = -.10, p < .05). Other self-help measures, including participation in an Operation Identification program, were not related to respondents' persistent feelings of fear.

Effects of Global Crime Prevention Activity

The main focus of this research was on assessing the effects of precautionary behavior and program participation constructed as global crime prevention measures, i.e., as summated indices. Both "direct effects" and "moderating effects" were examined. By direct effects we refer to the effects of precaution and program participation on fear of crime for the entire sample, which is generalizable to Kentucky's general population. By moderating effects, we refer to the effects of a third variable, e.g., victimization, on the relationship between two other variables, e.g., relationship between precaution and fear of crime (Baron & Kenny, 1986). In analysis of variance (ANOVA) terms, a basic moderator effect can be represented as an interaction between an independent variable, e.g., precaution, and another variable, e.g., victimization, that specifies the appropriate conditions for its operation.[2] Table 5.3 presents the bivariate correlations and multivariate correlations between measures of fear of crime, vulnerability measures, precaution, program participation, victimization, and moderator variables.

An examination of the direct effects of precautionary behavior and program participation that occur in the first six months (i.e., immediate effects) reveals that both significantly correlate with fear at Wave 1 (Beta = .26, p < .001; Beta = -.15, p < .05; respectively). Further, the analysis shows that household criminal victimization did not moderate the effects of precautionary behavior or crime prevention program participation on the fear of crime among the respondents of the panel study. It should be noted that these types of data do not allow us to conclude that precaution or crime prevention participation caused increases or decreases in fear, but simply that those who use more self-help measures reported higher levels of fear than other respondents and those who participated in more crime prevention programs had lower levels of fear. Although this fear may or may not have been caused or ameliorated by crime prevention actions, we can say that it is not accounted for by any differences between victims and non-victims, personal characteristics (age, gender, and education), lifestyle characteristics of the respondents (place of residence and employment status), or household characteristics (presence of other adults and children).

Table 5.3
The Effects of Precautionary Behavior, Program Participation and Victimization on Fear and the Persistence of Fear: Results from Multiple Regression Analysis

Variable(s) Entered	Fear (Wave 1)		Fear (Wave 2)	
	r	beta	r	beta
Fear W1	NA	NA	.78***	.72***
Vulnerability Measures				
Age	-.02	-.06	-.01	.02
Education	-.22***	-.25***	-.20***	-.02
Residence	.08	.02	.12	.05
Gender	-.21***	-.19***	-.22***	-.07
Number of adults	.05	.04	.07	.08
Number of children	.02	-.05	.00	-.09
Employment status	-.08	-.02	-.06	.02
Precaution W1	.24***	.26***	.21***	.05
Program Participation W1	.01	-.15*	-.02	-.03
Victimization Measures				
Victimization W1	.21***	.17**	.20***	.02
Victimization W2	NA	NA	.23***	.10**
Moderating Effects				
Pw1 x PPw1	.04	.08	.01	-.01
Pw1 x Vw1	.12	.02	.13*	.03
PPw1 x Vw1	.04	.01	.02	-.02
Pw1 x Vw2	NA	NA	.02	-.04
PPw1 x Vw2	NA	NA	.06	.04
Pw1 x Fw1	NA	NA	.08	.04
PPw1 x Fw1	NA	NA	-.05	-.03
R^2		.20		.64
(df)		(13,331)		(17,327)

Notes: *   p < .05
          **   p < .01
          *** p < .001

For assessing short-term effects of precautionary behavior and participation in crime prevention programs (six months to one year), fear at Wave
2 (Fear W2) was the dependent variable. The regression of Fear W2 was
comparable to the regression of Fear W1, except that Fear W1,
Victimization W2, and their interactions with precaution and program participation variables were included in the final equation.

In the regression of Fear W2, Fear W1 explained 52 percent of the
variance (i.e., persistence of fear). Neither precaution nor participation in
operation identification program at Wave 1 had an effect on the fear of
crime at Wave 2. In addition, there was no moderator effect of program
participation (i.e., the interaction between precaution and program participation) on the relationship between precaution and fear of crime (Pw1 x
PPw1 effect is specified in Table 5.3). Further, victimization at Wave 1 or
Wave 2 did not moderate the relationship between precaution at Wave 1 and
fear of crime at Wave 2 (Pw1 x Vw1 effect; Pw1 x Vw2 effect) or the relationship between program participation at Wave 1 and fear of crime at
Wave 2 (PPw1 x Vw1 effect; PPw1 x Vw2 effect). There were also no
moderator effects of Wave 1 fear on the relationship between precaution at
Wave 1 and fear at Wave 1 (Pw1 x Fw1 effect; PPw1 x Fw1 effect).

This pattern suggests that the relationship of the independent variables
to fear at Wave 2 is explained by their relationships to fear measured six
months earlier, with no further increases or decreases in fear attributable to
them. The nature of the persistence of fear six months later is that the level
of fear associated with it at Wave 1 of the study was maintained over the
following six months. Further, it was found that victims who had practiced
high precaution abandoned their fear no more rapidly than victims who had
not.

IMPLICATIONS FOR PROGRAM DEVELOPMENT
AND FUTURE RESEARCH

Program Development Implications

The results of this study reinforce previous Kentucky SAC research that
the law enforcement policy of promoting self-help preventive measures
would have to be judged as an insufficient solution to the problems of the
fear of crime. There was evidence that victims were more fearful than nonvictims up to one year later. However, no evidence was found that more
cautious victims fared better psychologically in the long run than did less
cautious victims. These "no significant effects" were found even when
including self-help precautionary measures (e.g., use of deadbolt locks) that
were left out of the earlier study. Perhaps a previous claim was correct in

that strictly individualized precautionary measures do little to promote a sense of security. They may make the home secure, but they do not decrease the level of perceived local danger. Rather than reduce fear, they actually may remind the occupants of the danger that lurks outside. Alarms, locks, and the like simply make the threat of crime more salient (Kidder & Cohn, 1979).

In addition to replicating the findings of an earlier SAC study, this study found that victims who were using self-help crime precaution measures in collaboration with a formal crime prevention program after the first incident were no less fearful than nonvictims or other victims who did not participate in a crime prevention program. The particular programs that were included in the present study were Operation Identification, Neighborhood Watch, and Crime Prevention Specialists Assistance. Unfortunately, the individual effects of the Neighborhood Watch and professional assistance programs could not be assessed because of their limited use.

There have been reports that perhaps crime prevention programs designed to increase caution may inadvertently increase fear. The conclusions of one study in particular suggested that if the reduction of fear is the goal of an intervention, information about the need for security measures must be coupled with reassurance that the recommended behaviors do, in fact, reduce one's vulnerability to crime (Norton & Courlander, 1982).

The inability of individuals to create a safe environment for themselves points to a need to focus their attention on alternative fear-reducing strategies. Two strategies proposed by the earlier SAC report bear repeating: "community building" and "physical rebuilding"—concepts that have been discussed for years in criminal justice. In general, these strategies attack the problems of fear of crime at the neighborhood or community level rather than at the personal or household level.

The former strategy of "community building" refers to efforts, primarily police practices, that attempt to enhance social cohesion in an urban environment. Previous research has shown that fear of crime is less prominent where persons are concerned about others, are confident that others are concerned about them, or are simply acquainted with one another. Projects promoting a sense that the police care or involving the police and residents in solving neighborhood problems appear to be effective descendants of the earlier "team-policing" concept designed to overcome police-resident isolation. More recently, the National Institute of Justice has sponsored experiments focusing on problem-oriented policies that required closer working relationships between the police and the community (Angell, 1975; Cordner, 1986; Henig & Maxfield, 1978; National Advisory Commission, 1976; Pate et al., 1986; Spelman & Eck, 1987; Waller, 1987).

The National Crime Prevention Council cites strategies that heighten the role of the police in information sharing and interagency cooperation. Law enforcement agencies in Jacksonville, Florida and Clifton, New Jersey are two that are engaging in comprehensive program development focusing on crime prevention through interagency communication and cooperation (National Crime Prevention Council, 1988a;1988b).

The latter strategy of "physical rebuilding" (improving lighting, removing blind spots, establishing communal areas, and promoting the circulation of people) is believed to reduce not only crime but also fear of crime in urban areas. People also respond with fear to signs of poverty and deterioration (e.g., abandoned housing); eliminating such symbols may be effective in reducing the perceived danger of urban environments (Jeffery, 1971; Kidder & Cohn, 1979; Newman, 1972).

These strategies are not independent. Alterations of the physical environment may enhance social cohesion. One research team evaluated the impact of physical changes on an urban neighborhood, such as cul-de-sacs and new traffic patterns, and found that residents used the neighborhood more often, intervened on behalf of one another more often, and were more likely to perceive their neighbors as a resource. Although change could not be attributed to the intervention, fear of crime in this neighborhood was significantly lower than would be expected, given citywide trends (Fowler & Mangione, 1982).

Implications for Future Research

The study presented here has several advantages over most previous studies on this topic. Its longitudinal design (two interviews, six months apart) allowed measures of precaution and program participation to be taken, and assessments made six months later, of respondents' level of fear, after controlling for previous fear. Further, the sample was drawn from a general statewide population; therefore, the findings relating to precautionary behavior are assessed as they occur naturally in the population. This sample of a statewide population also reveals findings reflecting participation in crime prevention programs in urban and rural America.

Most previous studies of precautionary measures have evaluated the effects of specific interventions where neighborhoods or groups were targeted for promotional activities in combination with other crime prevention activities. Although the findings here should be more generalizable than those from confined interventions, they cannot be considered complete in themselves. Several suggestions for future research on the subject are as follows.

First, a study should be conducted of precautionary behavior as it occurs naturally in the general population which includes measures of the *extent* of the precautionary behavior as well as the scope of the behavior. In other words, for each behavior respondents would be asked the extent to which they used self-help measures or participated in crime prevention programs rather than simply asking them a yes-no question. Measuring the extent of behavior may produce a more valid measure of a general precautionary behavior construct.

Second, there should be an examination of the use of self-help measures in the general population as they relate to the particular crimes which these measures are designed to prevent. This would mean that a panel study should be conducted which

> (1) first matched crime victims by type of crime and type of precautionary behavior (if any), and then

> (2) followed these crime victims for several years to assess their revictimization and level of fear of crime.

Third, a demonstration project should be conducted which

> (1) identifies crime victims (possibly victims of particular violent crimes and property crimes) in the general population, and

> (2) targets an intervention to persuade these victims to begin participating in particular crime prevention activities.

The study would follow these victims for several years, as well as a control group consisting of victims of the same type of crime but who were not involved in the crime prevention intervention.

CONCLUSIONS

This study found that self-initiated precautionary measures, as presently practiced, do little to reduce the level of fear of being victimized. This is the second Kentucky SAC study that has produced this result. Moreover, programs whose aim is, in part, to promote the use of self-help measures appear to show little promise of becoming a sufficient law enforcement policy response to the issue of fear of crime. It is true that campaigns to increase protective measures at the individual or household level are the easiest crime prevention programs to carry out by law enforcement agencies. It is also true that, compared to many other strategies, they take little time, money, or coordinated effort. But we found that they do nothing to reduce the perceived danger of an environment in which crime victims reside.

We advise caution in interpreting these findings, particularly as they relate to specific self-help measures. We are not recommending that people stop using deadbolt locks. We are recommending that criminal justice officials, particularly law enforcement officials, thoughtfully and critically reevaluate their current crime prevention policies and programs. These findings appear to justify, if not demand, the allocation of additional funds for the study of the effects of self-help measures and participation in formal programs with attention being given to crime victims.

NOTES

[1]   Two additional measures of age (under 55 = 0, over 55 = 1; and under 25 = 0, over 25 = 1) were created to check for possible curvilinear relationships between age and fear of crime. The correlation of these dummy variables with fear was as weak as the correlation of age and fear when treating age as a continuous measure.

[2]   Interaction terms were constructed by multiplying the difference of an independent variable from its mean and the difference of the third variable from its mean, i.e., $(x - x)$ $(z - z)$. See Pedhazur (1982) for a discussion of this procedure.

REFERENCES

American Psychological Association (1984). *Task Force on the Victims of Crime and Violence*. Final report. Washington, DC: author.

Angell, J.E. (1975). "The Democratic Model Needs a Fair Trial: Angell's Response." *Criminology*, 12,4:379-384.

Bard, M. & D. Sangrey (1986). *The Crime Victims' Book*. Secaucus, NJ: Citadel Press.

Baron, R.M. & D.A. Kenny (1986). "The Moderator-Mediator Variable Distinction in Social Psychological Research: Conceptual, Strategic, and Statistical Considerations." *Journal of Personality and Social Psychology*, 51,6:1173-1182.

Brown, L. (1984). "Strategies to Reduce the Fear of Crime." *The Police Chief*, 51:45-46.

Bureau of Justice Statistics (1986). *Annual Report Fiscal 1986*. Washington, DC: U.S. Department of Justice.

Cirel, P., P. Evans, D. McGillis & D. Whitcomb (1977). *Community Crime Prevention: An Exemplary Project, Seattle, WA*. Washington, DC: National Institute of Law Enforcement and Criminal Justice.

Cook, R., B. Smith & A. Harrell (1987). *Helping Crime Victims: Levels of Trauma and Effectiveness of Services*. Washington, DC: U.S. Department of Justice.

Cordner, G. (1986). "Fear of Crime and the Police: An Evaluation of a Fear-Reduction Strategy." *Journal of Police Science and Administration*, 14:223-233.

"Crime Prevention Measures at Household Level Found Futile" (1987). *Criminal Justice Newsletter*, 18,12(June):6.

Duncan, J.T. (1980). *Citizen Crime Prevention Tactics*. Washington, DC: National Institute of Justice.

Fowler, F. & T. Mangione (1982). *Neighborhood Crime, Fear, and Social Control: A Second Look at the Hartford Program.* Washington, DC: National Institute of Justice.

Henig, J. & M. Maxfield (1978). "Fear of Crime: Strategies for Intervention." *Victimology: An International Journal,* 3:297-313.

International Association of Chiefs of Police (1987). Conversation with Chairperson of the Crime Prevention Committee of the International Association of Chiefs of Police.

Janoff-Bulman, R. & I.A. Frieze (1983). "Theoretical Perspective for Understanding Reactions to Victimization." *Journal of Social Issues,* 39:1-17.

Jeffery, C.R. (1971). *Crime Prevention Through Environmental Design.* Beverly Hills, CA: Sage Publications.

Johnson, K. (1980). *A Multifaceted Evaluation of the Monterey County Burglary Prevention Unit.* Fairfax, VA: International Training, Research, and Evaluation Council.

_____ , F. Norris & L. Burgess (1986). *Criminal Victimization in Kentucky: A Longitudinal Study.* Louisville, KY: Urban Studies Center, Kentucky Criminal Justice Statistical Analysis Center, University of Louisville.

_____ & P. Hardyman (1987). *A Crime Estimation Program for Kentucky: Description and Preliminary Analysis.* Louisville, KY: Urban Studies Center, Kentucky Criminal Justice Statistical Analysis Center, University of Louisville.

Kaplan, H.M., L.E. Palkovitz & E.J. Pesce (1978). *Crime Prevention Through Environmental Design: Final Report on Residential Demonstration,* Minneapolis, Minnesota. Arlington, VA: Westinghouse Electric Corporation.

Kelling, G., T. Pate, D. Dieckman & C. Brown (1974). *The Kansas City Preventive Patrol Experiment: A Technical Report.* Washington, DC: Police Foundation.

Kidder, L. & E. Cohn (1979). "Public Views of Crime and Crime Prevention." In I.H. Frieze, D. Bar-Tal & J. Carroll (eds.) *New Approaches to Social Problems.* San Francisco: Jossey-Bass.

Lavrakas, P. (1985). "Citizen Self-Help and Neighborhood Crime Prevention Policy." In L. Curtis (ed.) *American Violence and Public Policy.* New Haven, CT: Yale University Press.

Lehnen, R.G. & W.G. Skogan (eds.) (1981). *The National Crime Survey: Working Papers, Volume I—Current and Historical Perspectives* (December, NCJ-75374). Washington, DC: U.S. Department of Justice, Bureau of Justice Statistics.

Lindsay, B. & D. McGillis (1986). "Citywide Community Crime Prevention: An Assessment of the Seattle Program." In D.P. Rosenbaum (ed.) *Community Crime Prevention: Does it Work?* Beverly Hills, CA: Sage Publications.

Lurigio, A.J. & D.P. Rosenbaum (1986). "Evaluation Research in Community Crime Prevention: A Critical Look at the Field." In D.P. Rosenbaum (ed.) *Community Crime Prevention: Does it Work?* Beverly Hills, CA: Sage Publications.

Miller, L. (1988). "Crime Prevention Commentary: Do Self-Help Measures Really Work?" *Crime Prevention News,* (Winter):9-10.

National Advisory Commission on Criminal Justice Standards and Goals (1976) *Task Force on Police.* Washington, DC: Department of Justice.

National Crime Prevention Council (1988a). *Catalyst* (March).

———— (1988b). *Catalyst* (April).

Newman, O. (1972). *Defensible Space: Crime Prevention Through Urban Design.* New York: MacMillan Press.

Norris, F. & K.W. Johnson (1987). *The Effects of Self-Help Precautionary Measures on Criminal Victimization and Fear: Implications for Crime Prevention Policy.* Washington, DC: U.S. Department of Justice, Bureau of Justice Statistics.

———— (1988). "The Effects of Self-Help Precautionary Measures on Criminal Victimization and Fear: Implications for Crime Prevention Policy." *Journal of Urban Affairs* 10,2:161-181.

Norton, L. & M. Courlander (1982). "Fear of Crime Among the Elderly—The Role of Crime Prevention Programs. *Gerontologist,* 22:388-393.

Pate, A.M., M.A. Wycoff, W.G. Skogan & L.W. Sherman (1986). *Reducing Fear of Crime in Houston and Newark: A Summary Report.* Washington, DC: Police Foundation.

Pedhazur, E. (1982). *Multiple Regression in Behavioral Research.* New York: Holt, Rinehart & Winston.

Police Foundation (1981). *The Newark Foot Patrol Experiment.* Washington, DC: author.

President's Task Force on Victims of Crime, Final Report. (1982). Washington, DC: Government Printing Office.

Skogan, W.G. (1986). "The Impact of Victimization on Fear." *Crime & Delinquency,* 33,1:135-155.

_____ & M. Maxfield (1981). *Coping with Crime: Individual and Neighborhood Reactions.* Beverly Hills, CA: Sage Publications.

Spelman, W. & J.E. Eck (1987). *Newport News Tests Problem-Oriented Policing.* Washington, DC: U.S. Department of Justice.

U.S. Department of Justice (1983). *Report to the Nation on Crime and Justice, the Data.* Washington, DC: Bureau of Justice Statistics.

U.S. Department of Justice (1986). *Criminal Victimization in the United States, 1984: A National Crime Survey Report.* Washington, DC: Bureau of Justice Statistics.

Urban Studies Center (1986). *How Many Kentuckians: Population Forecasts 1980-2020.* Louisville, KY: University of Louisville.

Waksberg, J. (1978). "Sampling Methods for Random-Digit Dialing." *Journal of the American Statistical Association,* 75:40-46.

Waller, I. (1976). "Victim Research, Public Policy, and Criminal Justice." *Victimology,* 1:240-252.

Whitaker, C. (1986). *Crime Prevention Measures.* Washington, DC: U.S. Department of Justice, Bureau of Justice Statistics.

Section II

POLICE ADMINISTRATION

Police administrative activities are crucial to successful police performance, despite the fact that they do not include direct service delivery to the public. Obviously, patrol cannot succeed without the right kinds of personnel; criminal investigation requires proper equipment; effective handling of domestic violence depends on training and clear policy; and so on. Police administrative functions enable police operations to be carried out.

In the first chapter in this section, Bob Langworthy discusses police organizational structure. Logically, this is an important initial concern, because all else takes place within the constraints established by organizational structure. Langworthy provides an historical analysis of police department structure, as well as a complete review of research on structure from the general organization theory literature. In his chapter, more so than in most, it becomes clear that determining the best structure depends on first being able to specify goals and objectives, something we are often not able to do in policing. Consequently, the answer to the question, "What police organizational structure works best?" can only be, "It all depends." Langworthy provides considerable insight on what it is that it all depends. This information should prove helpful in the selection of the most appropriate structure, given a set of objectives and work-related characteristics.

Next, Larry Gaines and Vic Kappeler give an overview of legal considerations, research, and issues pertaining to police selection and testing. This is an especially important topic, since policing is a very labor-intensive business and selection and testing largely determine who the laborers will be. Over the last few decades, these have been two of the aspects of police administration most affected by federal legislation, appellate court decisions, and civil suits. Gaines and Kappeler provide a concise summary of current legal restrictions, although readers should be aware that this is a fast-changing area of the law. The authors also discuss current practice and research relating to such selection techniques as written, physical fitness, and psychological tests, as well as to employment qualifications pertaining to vision, education, and drug use.

In "Women in Policing," Donna Hale traces the progress of women in American policing since their entry into police departments in the early 1900s. Based on a review of the literature, she concludes that there are few differences in the performance of men and women on patrol, and that the public seems largely to accept and support the complete integration of women into policing. The major obstacle that women encounter in policing is from male police officers and managers. She concludes the chapter with recommendations from earlier studies on how police departments can best accomplish complete gender integration.

In the next chapter, Keith Haley provides a succinct examination of past and present practices in police training. He points out the important role played by the Law Enforcement Assistance Administration (LEAA) in the development of basic police training during the 1970s and 1980s. He also identifies the major impact that Police Officer Standards and Training (POST) councils have had on establishing and later upgrading minimum police training and selection standards in the states. Haley describes current developments emanating from the emphasis on performance objectives, from developments of various kinds in instructional technology, and from civil liability concerns. Perhaps most importantly, he stresses that although we often seem to see training as a kind of panacea for correcting police problems, we have almost no empirical research on the actual effects of training on police performance.

The final chapter by Mittie Southerland and Elizabeth Reuss-Ianni provides a thorough review of research on leadership and management effectiveness. Although there have been thousands of studies of leadership and management in private and public organizations, there have been only a few in police agencies, and these have mostly dealt with self-perceptions and subordinate preferences, rather than truly focusing on what works. The non-police research indicates that the most effective leadership and management practices vary from one situation to the next. Southerland and Reuss-Ianni consider the application of this body of research to policing situations, and they discuss the increasingly popular topics of organizational values and organizational culture. They conclude that values and culture are particularly important determinants of behavior in police organizations, and discuss how police agencies might exert more influence than they presently do over these important matters.

6

Organizational Structure

Robert H. Langworthy
University of Cincinnati

INTRODUCTION

The simple answer to the question, "Which police organizational structures work?" is that they all work and they all work equally well. A more useful answer, however, is that while all structures work and work equally well, they do not all work equally well in all situations. This chapter explores alternative police organizational structures by first describing the alternatives and noting the suitability of each. The discussion continues with the difficulty we have in empirically determining which structure is "best" for police. This discussion turns on the distinction between empirical and normative issues noting that decisions concerning what works (i.e., what is best) are normative concerns that cannot be addressed empirically. The chapter concludes by providing a framework that may prove a useful aid in helping decide which organizational structure is appropriate in a given situation.

WHAT ARE THE ALTERNATIVES?

The focus of this chapter is on the formal structure of police organizations. However, because there is considerable debate in the literature that juxtaposes formal and informal organizational structures, a few comments seem warranted. Organizational structures can be viewed as stable patterns of interaction between persons or positions within an organization. These stable patterns of interaction can be prescribed by the organization (formal organizational structures) or they can emerge naturally as do friendships and cliques (informal organizational structures). Roberg (1979) contrasts the two structures noting that formal structures are created by the organization to achieve organizational goals. Informal structures, by contrast, emerge "naturally" and focus on achieving the goals of the group.

While it is widely acknowledged that the informal organizational structure exerts considerable influence on the productivity of an organization, this chapter focuses on the formal structure, which places organizational actors in proximity to one another and gives them the opportunity to interact both formally and informally. While an agency's formal organizational structure clearly shapes its informal organizational structure, the opposite effect seems less likely. Simply put, rearranging the organizational chart will alter the informal structure, whereas changes in the informal structure are not likely to change the organizational chart.[1]

The dominant characterization of structural alternatives comes from the work of Burns and Stalker (1961). In their study of British manufacturing firms Burns and Stalker identified two types of organizational structures: mechanistic and organic. While there are a number of assumptions that attend this distinction, the structures themselves are rather simply distinguished. Mechanistic structures are characterized as complex vertically (hierarchical) and horizontally (division of labor), whereas organic structures are characterized as vertically and horizontally simple or undifferentiated.

However, the fact that there are different organizational forms begs the question—which one is best? The question has not been lost on organizational theorists, and all of them have an answer. Classical theorists of the early 1900s promoted the mechanistic model, while the neo-classicists or human relations theorists of the mid-1900s favored the organic model. Beginning with the work of Burns and Stalker (1961) and elaborated by Woodward (1965) there appeared a shift from universal support for either the mechanistic or organic models to a more reasoned situational or contingency perspective.

Contingency theorists suggest that the organizational situation conditions the appropriateness of the organizational structure. Burns and Stalker found a relation between environmental stability and structure while Woodward isolated a relationship between the nature of the technology of manufacturing firms and organizational structure. Burns and Stalker concluded that organizations operating in stable environments were most efficient when they were mechanistic, whereas firms in unstable environments were most efficient if organically structured. Woodward noted that successful manufacturing firms employing routine technologies tended to be mechanistically structured, whereas, firms employing custom and nonroutine technologies were more likely to be successful if they were organically structured.

Debates surrounding police organizational structure have evolved in much the same manner as the general organizational literature. Early police organizational theorists favored the mechanistic style of organization. Beginning in the mid-1960s a number of theorists began to favor organic models, while more recently contingency models have begun to emerge.

Early Police Organization[2]

With the advent of paid municipal police in the mid-1800s came the necessity of creating organizations to provide police service. Early on, police organizations were radically decentralized, reflecting their close ties to political machines and ward politics. The agenda for these police organizations was to do a minimum amount of law enforcement, keep the neighborhood relatively quiet, and serve the needs of entrenched political interests. This organizational mission was well served by a decentralized organizational structure, for it accommodated the cultural diversity of American cities and recognized the technological inability of organizations to regulate the behavior of police from a central authority.

At about the turn of the century there was a shift in the political climate in America. Political reformers tiring of the particularistic practices of political machines sought to reform politics. To do so they attacked the alliance between politics and the police. The attack on the police, while focusing on severing the relation between police and politics, advocated adoption of the mechanistic or bureaucratic model for police organizational structure. It was suggested that the bureaucratic model would bring the police under central control and regulate police practices. Central administrative control was thus considered the vehicle through which control of the police could be wrested from politicians (particularly ward leaders) thereby fostering better police services.

Another characteristic of the reform agenda was reflected in changes in the police mission. In the effort to carve out a niche to which police could lay claim to "professional" expertise the reformers sought to limit the role of police to law enforcement. The emergent legalistic focus, and its attendant deemphasis on service and order, resulted in a mission that could be characterized as routine.

Reformer sponsorship of the mechanistic form for police organizations was consistent with both of these planks of the reform agenda. First, bureaucratic organizational structures served to insulate police from politics, making it possible to reform politics without having to deal with machine muscle. Second, the reformers' conception of the proper police mission, routine processing of law violators, would be most efficiently handled by a mechanistic organizational structure. Thus, the bureaucratic organizational structure proposed by the turn of the century reformers was consistent with their view of the proper role of the police and with their desire to witness a separation of police and politics.

During the period between the turn of the century and the early 1960s the reformers enjoyed remarkable success in altering the public conception of what the police ought to do and how they ought to be organized. This period of reform witnessed the displacement of patronage with civil service, divesture of regulatory services (licensing and inspections) that allowed greater focus on law enforcement, and both technological and organizational innovation that made it possible to centralize police command and control. The reformers were also successful in restricting the role of police to law enforcement, wherein police became the dispassionate ministers of the law enacting "state" policy.

The Backlash

The reformers' success also spelled their failure. Police now functioning as ministers of the law and agents of the state were the focal point for blame for the civil unrest that plagued many American cities in the late 1960s and early 1970s. The inequities of the "state" were most clearly manifest when the "state" flexed its muscle; in other words when the "state" engaged the police to do its bidding. Thus, the police were held responsible for much of the civil unrest that characterized the era and there were calls on many fronts for radical reorganization of police agencies.

There were a number of elements that characterized the call for reorganization, but the two most important were the reconceptualization of the police mission and reform of police organizations. Where the turn-of-the-century reformers sought to restrict the police mission to law enforcement and to make police organizations mechanistic, the 1970s reformers sought to further expand the police role to include peacekeeping and service and to re-introduce the organic form of police organization (Figure 6.1 illustrates the changing police role). The 1970s reform movement is now just 20 years old but it is thriving. We have witnessed the evolution of abstract "democratic alternatives" to manifest team policing and the present-day community-oriented policing.

Figure 6.1
Contraction and Expansion of the Mission of Police
in America, 1850s to the 1980s

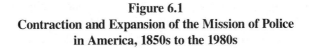

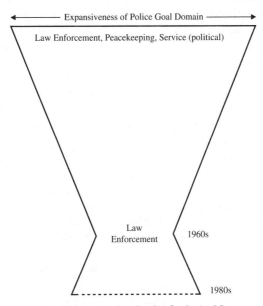

Law Enforcement, Peacekeeping, Service (social)

What we have also witnessed is a congruence of the conceptions of police mission and organizational structure. Just as the turn of the century reformers proposed a structure congruent with their conception of the police mission, so too have the 1970s reformers. The espoused mission of the current reformers is broader, including, as coequal elements, law enforcement, order maintenance, and provision of a broad range of municipal (if not social) services. This mission stands in sharp contrast to the mission adopted by the turn-of-the-century reformers and has dramatic implications for organizational structure. While we do not have much trouble defining behavior as legal or illegal, we do not possess the same ability to defend order or specify which social services fall within the purview of the police force. Even if we could define services and order, we would not have the luxury of an established technology (process) for converting disorderly situations into orderly situations or of knowing which service is appropriate when. Thus, the reinstated police mission does not allow routine application of known processes to accomplish organizational objectives. Indeed, the inclusive mission requires tailoring of solutions to changeable organizational goals. Organic, rather than mechanistic, organizational structures are best suited for dealing with changeable environmental elements that require the fashioning of unique solutions to achieve organizational objectives.

The rhetorical vacillation between mechanistic and organic models and their attendant conceptions of the police mission has led several authors to suggest that there is a middle ground. That is, it may be that different organizational structures are appropriate for different situations. The organizational contingency perspective, as applied in the police organizational literature, has focused on two themes (contingencies). First, Roberg (1979) and Kuykendall (Kuykendall & Roberg, 1982:243) adopted Burns & Stalker's environmental stability focus and Woodward's technology concern and concluded "that the degree to which a mechanistic police organization should move to more of an organic approach is also variable." The implication is that police organizational structures should fit environmental and technological exigencies.

In another contingency discussion, Cordner (1978) contrasts open (organic) and closed (mechanistic) models of police organization. Cordner notes, as did Roberg and Kuykendall, that closed structures are appropriate in stable, routine environments while open structures are appropriate in unstable environments where technologies are non-routine. What Cordner adds to the debate is recognition of the implications of these abstractions for police work. Cordner contends that the closed model is inappropriate for police organizations because police work is not routine nor does it occur in a stable environment. He also notes that though the open model is intended to operate in unstable non-routine environments, its focus on ends, with little or no regard for means, is antithetical to constitutional due process concerns. Cordner, though concluding that the open model is superior to the closed one, acknowledges that there are problems associated with both models. If a police organization must work in an unstable environment and use nonroutine technologies, then closed organizational models may not be appropriate. However, the decision to shift to an open model, with its ends orientation, may place individual liberties in jeopardy.

We now find ourselves in the position of contending that both waves of reformers, not to mention the initial efforts to organize police, had the proper organizational structure to accomplish the institutional agenda as it was then viewed. The problem is, if each of the organizational structures has been correct for the then fashionable conception of the organizational mission, then why have we rarely been satisfied with the police?

WHY CAN'T WE TELL A GOOD ORGANIZATION WHEN WE SEE IT?

There have been very few empirical studies of police organizational structure. The few studies that have been performed are basically of two types: those that describe manifest structures and those that try to isolate structures that are the "most" effective. If we try to use these studies to determine which police organizational structure is "best," we have to make a number of assumptions. If we use manifest structures as a guide to what is best, we must make a kind of Darwinian assumption that manifest organizational structures survive because they are effective. Our task then would be to determine what kinds of structures appear to survive in what kinds of environments. If we use efficiency or effectiveness as the criterion by which we determine the best organizational structure, the problem is one of specifying the efficiency or effectiveness criterion.

Manifest Structures

Studies that focus on manifest police organizational structures examine correlates of organizational structure with the implied promise of improving our understanding of why organizations are structured as they appear to be. These studies take the organizational structure as the dependent variable, developing or testing theories to explain why police are organized as they are. To use these studies as guides to what is best, we must assume that what survives is best.

One of the first to systematically examine police organizational structures was James Q. Wilson. His initial examination (1963) and later more complete treatise (1968) viewed police organizational structure as a product of political culture. Wilson's thesis was that political culture constrains police behavior and organizational structure. He suggested that the immigrant or caretaker political cultures were associated with watchman-style police organizational behavior and decidedly nonbureaucratic organizational structures. Yankee-Protestant or "good government" political cultures, by contrast, were associated with legalistic or service-style organizational behavior and bureaucratic organizational structures. Though Wilson did test his police behavior thesis, he did not test the constraint theory of organizational structure.

As part of a larger study, Langworthy (1986) examined the Wilson constraint theory of police organizational structure and found it wanting. Langworthy operationalized political culture in a manner logically consistent with Wilson's measurement of political culture and could find no evidence of a constraining effect on a variety of organizational structure variables.[3]

Langworthy also explored a number of other theoretically relevant correlates of organizational structure: size of the organization, technology employed by the organization (the working style of the organization), the complexity of the population (occupational and industrial), and the stability of the population. The overwhelming conclusion from this analysis was that there are no structural imperatives associated with the above-noted variables. Indeed, even when strong correlates were noted, ample variance remained, suggesting that these theoretically significant variables did not fundamentally determine police organizational structures.

A final study focused on the rank structure of police organizations. Guyot's (1979) examination of problems associated with the traditional police rank structure explored the relation between agency size and rank structure. She reached the conclusion that "the reader should see at a glance that size makes no systematic difference" (1979:255).

What these studies have revealed is that while there may be tendencies for some relations to prevail, there is no clear constraining effect of any variable, or set of variables explored to date, on police organizational structure. Thus, existent examinations of manifest structures fail to offer much in the way of helping us isolate the "best" police organizational structure. What is manifest is a broad range of organizational structures with the full range appearing in all environments.

Longitudinal studies, chronicling enduring police organizations, may offer historical insights concerning why those structures have lasted. Such studies may begin to develop a knowledge base from which we can address the question of "which structure is best?" from studies of manifest structures. We do not presently have that empirical knowledge base, and it does not seem likely that we will determine what is best from what is manifest.[4]

Effective Structures

Studies that have sought to isolate the most effective structures have typically focused on a very small, though significant, aspect of the police role—law enforcement. One noteworthy exception to this generalization is Sherman's (1980) "Causes of Police Behavior" review essay. Sherman sought to "organize and codify the findings of quantitative research on four aspects of police behavior: detection, arrest, service, and violence" (1980:69).

Of the approximately 85 empirical studies Sherman reviewed, 15 offered either intraorganizational or interorganizational explanations of police behavior. The only consistent police behavior/organizational structure correlate he isolated was a positive relation between agency arrest rates and bureaucratic organization. What is revealing in Sherman's review is the restricted range of efficiency or effectiveness criteria employed in empirical studies. Sherman was able to locate few studies that addressed his other concerns (efficiency in detection and service or control of police violence), and even in these few studies there was scant reference to structural correlates of police behavior.

Since the 1980 publication of Sherman's review essay, a number of authors have explored the relation between organizational structure and agency outputs. Allen (1982) noted that intensity of supervision marginally alters police officer behavior. Smith and Klein (1983) noted that bureaucratization had a modest positive relation to likelihood of an arrest. Further, the Smith and Klein analysis revealed that there was no relation between intensity of supervision and the likelihood of arrest. More recently, Slovak (1986) has shown that several features of organizational structure are related to arrest rates. Slovak's regression analyses yield positive regression coefficients between violent crime arrest rates and span of control, a positive coefficient between violent crime arrest rates and civilianization, and a positive coefficient between the property crime arrest rate and civilianization.

A synopsis of the empirical literature that attempts to link agency efficiency or effectiveness to organizational structure provides about as much insight as did the manifest structures literature. In point of fact, there is not much in the efficiency-effectiveness literature that suggests which of the police organizational structures is "best." About all that can be said is that the turn-of-the-century reformers may have been on to something. It would appear that their linking of bureaucracy to law enforcement bore fruit. To the extent that there is general support in the empirical literature for an organizational structure relation to agency outputs, it is that bureaucratic police organizations tend to produce more legalistic outputs (arrest rates, clearance rates, official referrals) than organic organizational structures.

The intriguing question, then, is why we are not satisfied with the bureaucratic model? After all, that organizational form was sold as a vehicle for producing law enforcement; presumably the law enforcement mission was bought along with the bureaucratic model. The bureaucratic police organization appears to have delivered law enforcement as promised, so why were the 1970s reformers disenchanted? The disaffection probably turns on different conceptions of the organizational goal of police.

If police goals change, as fashions do, then we must consider several issues in order to address concerns about which police organizational structures work best. First, we must determine whether it is possible to specify the "true" police organizational goal.[5] If it is possible to specify the "true" police organizational goal, then we will have the capacity to halt the ebb and flow of police organizational goal fashion swings by certifying the one true goal. Further, if we have a certified goal, we will have a vehicle for purposefully designing police organizations and a criterion for evaluating their performance.

If it is not possible to specify the one "true" police organizational goal, it may still be possible to specify many "true" police organizational goals. If we can isolate many "true" police organizational goals, then part of our problem is still solvable. If there are many "true" police organizational goals we will have to design many police organizations, being ever careful that we use the intended organizational goal as the evaluation criterion. The part of the problem that is not solvable is the ebb and flow of organizational goal fashionability, but even here tacit recognition that there are many "true" police organizational goals is helpful. If there are many "true" police organizational goals and if police organizational theory recognizes that there are many "true" police organizational goals, then we will have the capacity to nurture the evolution of many different police organizational structures, each tailored to achieve a particular conception of the police organizational goal.[6] Thus, if we are to understand police organizations from an efficiency perspective, the question remains whether there is one "true" police organizational goal that all police organizations serve, or many "true" conceptions of the police organizational goal served by many different police organizations?

THE CONCEPT OF A POLICE ORGANIZATIONAL GOAL

The preceding discussions have noted that reformers have linked mission and structure in a manner consistent with theory, and that empirical studies of manifest structures and structural efficiency have failed to provide us with much insight. In the first instance we note congruence between mission and structure but perpetual dissatisfaction with police and a continuous call for reorganization. Our review of the empirical research reveals only variety (no explanation of variation) and silence with regard to efficiency. Thus the question remains: Why can't we tell which organizational form is best for the police?

The answer may lie in our inability to specify the police organizational goal, because if we cannot specify what the organization is to achieve, we cannot specify the "best way to achieve it." There are two elements that interact to make specification of the police organizational goal difficult. First is the view that an organizational goal is not singular, but rather a multidimensional construct that must be satisfied in all its dimensions simultaneously (Duffee, 1980). Where police are concerned, this premise expressly rejects the notion that the police organizational goal is either law enforcement, service, or peacekeeping, arguing instead that police organizations are best viewed as serving all three dimensions of the organizational goal simultaneously. Thus, according to the multidimensional construct thesis, if a police organization were to satisfy its organizational goal, it would satisfy all three elements simultaneously.

The second issue, suggested by Mohr (1982), is that an organizational goal is a normative construct, that is, an organizational goal is not empirical. Mohr notes that theories of organizational efficiency are normative because there is no way to objectively determine which of the plausible organizational goals is the true goal. Mohr further complicates the issue by noting that even if an organizational goal could be agreed upon, its content (dimensions in the multidimensional construct discussion above) could not be. Finally, Mohr suggests that even if the true goal could be isolated and its content specified, there still would not be agreement as to which of the dimensions to emphasize or objective means for determining which prioritization of goal dimensions represents the "true" organizational goal.

A final problem isolated by Mohr (1982; see also Duffee, 1980) concerns goal exclusivity. Mohr observes that if an organization shares responsibility for goal achievement with other organizations or institutions, it will be increasingly difficult to determine whether the organization has successfully addressed its goal. Where the police are concerned, it is clear that they share their triadic goal with many different organizations and institutions. If we generalize law enforcement to norm enforcement, we see that most institutions of civil society share this goal. Schools, churches, family, etc. all are involved in norm enforcement. Peacekeeping is but another variant of norm enforcement that numerous institutions promote. Likewise, police fail to have a monopoly on service provision.[7] Thus, though the police organizational goal may well consist of law enforcement, peacekeeping, and service, the police share that organizational agenda with other organizations and institutions. A consequence of shared responsibility is that the organization cannot determine whether it is doing a good job. Simply put, the police may be doing a good job, while other organizations and institutions that share responsibility for the police organizational goal may be failing; the goal, thus, appears not to be met and the organization appears to be failing.

Within the context of this discussion, it is apparent that the reason we cannot tell a good police organization when we see one is that we cannot see one. That is, the evaluation criterion, the police organizational goal, is not empirical because it is too complex to be observable and because it is shared with other organizations and institutions. Thus, observations regarding goal satisfaction cannot be attributed. It may be that the conclusion regarding which police organizational form "works best" is indeed a normative conclusion beyond the purview of empirical social sciences. However, if we determine that conclusions regarding police organization are essentially normative, then we must simultaneously accept the fact that different normative orders may indeed conclude that different organizational forms are "best."

That decisions concerning police organizational structure are essentially normative and not empirical does not excuse decisionmakers from logical decision-making with full explication of the values (norms) on which decisions rest. In fact, as decisions become more normative and less empirical the values on which decisions rest become more important because they provide the only basis for evaluating resultant decisions.[8]

To date, police organization and reorganization decision-making has been done through a hazy logic that attempts to link a conception of the police organizational goal to organizational structure. The form of these arguments is that a particular organizational structure is best suited to a particular organizational goal without clear articulation of why one structure is superior to another given a particular goal. Where the linkage is formed on an empirical basis, we can simply test the presumption by analysis of the data. However, when the linkage is based on logic, we need as much insight into the logic employed as possible to insure that decisions and reviews of those decisions are as thorough as possible. The remainder of this chapter will be devoted to development of a logical system that links perceptions of organizational inputs to types of technologies needed to process inputs, and finally to structures that appear logically appropriate for housing those technologies.

THE PERROW FRAMEWORK

In 1967, Charles Perrow presented what he termed a framework for the comparative analysis of organizations. The framework grew out of work with colleagues (Street, Vinter & Perrow, 1966) and was elaborated on in subsequent work by Perrow (1970, 1979). The framework emerges from the interaction of two characteristics of raw input materials that have implications for the kinds of technologies that are employed to transform inputs to organizational outputs. The resultant technological typology then can be logically tied to organizational structures. The real value of the logical system is that it frames a number of questions that must be addressed before decisions concerning police organization can be rendered.

The Nature of Inputs

Perrow suggests that two characteristics of inputs are of paramount concern: (1) input variability and (2) the degree to which inputs are well understood. The first characteristic, input variability, is concerned with the degree to which inputs the organization receives for processing are all the same. Thus, inputs can be characterized as being more or less consistent. Inputs also can be characterized as being well or poorly understood. Inputs about which a great deal is known, or presumed known, can be characterized as well understood. Inputs about which there is little knowledge would be characterized as poorly understood.

Inputs to police organizations can be viewed as either stable or variable, well understood or poorly understood. If we focus on people inputs to police processing, we witness competing conceptions of people and how they should be treated. Constitutionally, police are supposed to treat people equally before the law, and thus inputs are stable or all the same. It also is plausible to argue that people are unique individuals. If the latter definition of inputs is employed, we must conclude that inputs are unstable or variable. Choice of police organizational goals has implications for which conception of people is served. If police are simple ministers of the law, then there is every expectation that people will be treated as if they are all the same. However, if police are to use discretion in keeping the peace or deciding which services to provide, there is every expectation that they will treat people differently depending upon situational exigencies. In the former situation inputs are stable, while in the latter inputs are variable.

Just as police organizational inputs can be defined as either stable or variable, so too can they be defined as well or poorly understood. Again, if police are viewed as ministers of the law, then it is quite conceivable that inputs can be characterized as well understood. Police survey the landscape and separate people into those who are breaking the law and those who are not. Police then deal with the lawbreakers, presuming to know all that is needed to insure that the goal, law enforcement, is addressed. Police providing services can be described as operating from a knowledge base (high degree of understanding) or they can be viewed as operating from an intuitive base (low degree of understanding). While police who provide services and keep the peace tend to deal with a broader range of inputs than police who focus on law enforcement, they can be instructed as to how to intervene in the variety of situations or they can be left to their own discretion. In the former case there is presumed knowledge of inputs that allows dictation of intervention strategies, whereas in the latter knowledge is presumed lacking, and intuition and experience are relied upon.

The Nature of Technology

Perrow logically derives the characteristics of technology from the characteristics of work inputs. The link is that the nature of the inputs influences the nature of the process for transforming inputs to work outputs. To summarize the relation, input variability and the frequency of exceptions encountered in the transformation process are positively related, as are level of understanding about how to transform inputs and the analyzability of work-related problems.

The relation between input variability and frequency of exceptions encountered by the technology is fairly unambiguous. If an industry has to process variable inputs, it will encounter and have to be able to handle frequent exceptions to standard practices. Likewise, if the industry processes stable inputs, the technology need not anticipate frequent exceptions, as inputs typically will be the same. However, the relation between degree of understanding and analyzability is not so straightforward. Analyzability refers to the nature of the search process when exceptions are encountered. If the search process is conducted in a logical and analytical manner, then analyzability is high. If, however, when problems appear or opportunities manifest themselves, the search is based on intuition, experience, or guesswork, the process is characterized as low on analyzability. The link between understanding and analyzability is the knowledge base. If a solid knowledge base exists and understanding of inputs is high, logical and analytical search processes can be engaged when exceptions are encountered. However, if the knowledge base is weak, then understanding of inputs is at a low level and the search for solutions to problems will be intuitive, based on experience, or simply guesswork.

Applying these concepts to police work, we again see that police work can be viewed as involving few exceptions (as when all inputs are the same or as when there is a limited police role) as well as a high degree of analyzability (as when officers act as ministers of the law or when policy guides all action). Conversely, police work can also be viewed as encountering frequent exceptions (as when all situations and individuals are treated as unique events) and analyzability can be seen as low (as when officers are expected to exercise considerable discretion).

The Comparative Framework

Perrow's framework emerges from the interaction of the characteristics of the technology. Perrow treats the characteristics as orthogonal to each other and creates a four-fold typology from their interaction. Figure 6.2 illustrates the typology derived from Perrow.

Figure 6.2
Perrow's Organizational Typology Resulting from Cross Classification of the Natures of Technology

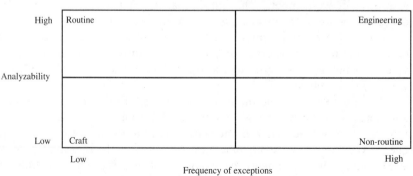

The four types of technology that emerge from the interaction are:

(1) *craft*, which encounters few exceptions but must rely on intuitive processes for problem solving;

(2) *routine*, which encounters few exceptions and uses analytical problem-solving methods;

(3) *engineering*, which encounters many exceptions and uses analytical problem solving; and

(4) *non-routine*, which encounters many exceptions but must rely on intuitive problem-solving processes.

What emerges from the typology is a conception of routine and nonroutine processes by which inputs are transformed to outputs. In both the routine and engineering cells the technology is routinely engaged. The distinction between the two is that in the engineering cell another step has to be added; a step that acts like a sorter which sorts the inputs into groups of raw materials that can subsequently be processed routinely. The craft and non-routine cells, by contrast, cannot rely upon routine processes for processing exceptions because these technologies are processing material about which there is a dearth of knowledge. When exceptions are encountered in craft and non-routine technologies, problem solving takes the form of the individual or collective best guess based on intuition or experience but not on logical, analytical application of the knowledge base.

The police technological analog to Perrow is found by coupling Wilson's depiction of varieties of police behavior with the concept of team policing.[9] Perrow's routine cell is analogous to Wilson's legalistic style of police behavior. Legalistic police departments view their work as law enforcement (low input variety, low frequency of exceptions) about which there is clear guidance concerning behaviors that are illegal and clear instructions regarding what is to be done if illegal behavior is observed (engage the prosecution process with regard for due process). Service-style police departments employ technologies analogous to Perrow's engineering. Service-style police organizations get involved in a broad range of activities but with clear direction from the community in articulated policy. Thus, service-style and legalistic policing represent routine processing of varied inputs on the one hand and invariate inputs on the other; neither, however, requires or promotes the exercise of discretion.

The craft police analog is watchman-style policing. In the watchman style, police rarely encounter exceptions, but when they do, problem solving is left to personal discretion based on experience and intuition. Team policing is the non-routine analog. Agencies that employ team policing engage their officers in a broad range of municipal services but rely on the team to collectively fashion solutions to problems. The problem-solving methodology employed here is collegial problem solving, which involves collective experience, intuition, or best guessing. In both of these latter types of technologies the dearth of knowledge or lack of dicta results in the exercise of discretion based on intuition and experience for problem solving rather than on consultation of a body of knowledge.

Structural Correlates of Technology

At this point we are in a position to attach structural correlates to the technologies. The service- and legalistic-style police organizations have a knowledge base either in the law and in due process or in dicta (policy) that seems to make discretion disappear. Mechanistic structures are designed expressly to minimize the exercise of discretion, hence it seems that both legalistic- and service-style police departments should be mechanistically structured. Watchman and team police styles, by contrast, lack the knowledge base to rely on routine processing and hence must facilitate officer exercise of discretion. In these settings where decision-making is based on individual or collective experience and intuition, organic organizations would seem to be the most appropriate.

This chapter began with the observation that all police organizational structures work and work equally well, but suggested that the important question concerned in what circumstances particular structures are superior to others. The discussion then turned to a review of efforts to unearth circumstances that seemed to favor one organizational form over another. These efforts focused on historical analyses of police organizational theories, empirical studies of manifest organizational structures, and theories of police organizational efficiency. The overwhelming conclusion is that we have not learned a great deal from empirical studies about contingencies favoring one police organizational form over another.

The failure of empirical studies to provide guidance was then attributed to the possibility that police organizational efficiency is not an empirical question because we cannot objectively specify the evaluation criterion—the organizational goal. It was then suggested that because we cannot determine empirically which organizational form is best, the normative logic underpinning police organization and reorganization decisions is all the more important. The crux of this argument is that the only means of evaluating normative decisions is by examination of the logic supporting the decisions whereas empirically based decisions can be evaluated by examining the data.

Perrow's framework was then introduced as a vehicle for structuring police organizational decision-making. Perrow's framework leads one logically from a perception of input materials, to a typification of technologies, and finally, to correlated structures. The real value in the Perrow framework is that it forces organization designers to consider their conception of inputs as the base point from which to develop organization and reorganization recommendations.

If the question "Which police organizational structure works best?" is considered within the Perrow framework, the answer is that it depends on the nature of inputs to the police organization. If police are viewed as ministers of the law or as ministers of the local will, then a mechanistic organizational structure that curbs discretion and insures that either the law or local will is routinely served is best. However, if police are viewed as craftspersons or professionals who are expected to use their individual or collective judgments, then organic structures which promote discretion are best.

NOTES

[1] It is plausible to argue that if there is too much dissonance between formal and informal structures, that formal structures will have to be reformed to recognize exigencies of the work.

[2] This discussion borrows liberally from Fogelson (1977), Walker (1977), and Monkkenon (1981).

[3] Langworthy (1985) also reexamined Wilson's test of the constraint theory on police organizational behavior and while replicating Wilson's central tendency theory could find no evidence to support the constraint theory of behavior.

[4] We must remember that "what is best" is a normative question while "what is manifest" is an empirical question.

[5] The phrase "police organizational goal" refers to a multidimensional construct variously described as a set of organizational goals consisting of testors and generators (Simon, 1964; Duffee, 1980) or transitive and reflexive elements (Mohr, 1973; Langworthy, 1989). The concept of an organizational goal is developed more fully in the following section.

[6] There is a third possibility. It is logically possible that police agencies do not have an organizational goal. While this is logically possible it does not seem plausible. Publicly funded municipal police organizations have been in existence in America for over 140 years. It does not seem likely that organizations formed, reformed, and reformed yet again would have endured that long without a goal. Organizations without a goal may be formed, but they are not likely to survive and it is even less likely that they will be reformed. Given that police agencies have endured and that most have even been reorganized, it seems likely that they serve a purpose.

7   Wilson, in his discussion of police as service providers, notes that others are available to provide services that police provide and that it is really beyond the realm of police responsibility to provide services (1968:4-5).

8   If decisions are based on empirical rationales, examination of the decisions can be accomplished simply by looking at the data (see Langworthy, 1986).

9   See Cordner and Greene (1983) for a broader criminal justice system application of the Perrow framework.

REFERENCES

Allen, D. (1982). "Police Supervision on the Street: An Analysis of Supervisor/Officer Interaction During the Shift." *Journal of Criminal Justice,* 10:91-109.

Burns, B. & G. Stalker (1961). *The Management of Innovation.* London: Tavistock.

Cordner, G. (1978). "Open and Closed Models of Police Organization: Traditions, Dilemmas, and Practical Considerations." *Journal of Police Science and Administration,* 6: 22-34.

_____ & J. Greene (1983). "Book Review Essay: Policy and Administration in Criminal Justice Organizations." In W. Jones, Jr. (ed.) *Criminal Justice Administration,* pp. 101-133. New York: Marcel Dekker.

Duffee, D. (1980). *Correctional Management: Change and Control in Correctional Agencies.* Englewood Cliffs, NJ: Prentice-Hall.

Fogelson, R. (1977). *Big City Police.* Cambridge: Harvard University Press.

Guyot, D. (1979). "Bending Granite: Attempts to Change the Rank Structure of American Police Departments." *Journal of Police Science and Administration,* 7:253-284.

Kuykendall, J. and R. Roberg (1982). "Mapping Police Organizational Change: From a Mechanistic Toward an Organic Model." *Criminology,* 20:241-256.

Langworthy, R. (1985). "Wilson's Theory of Police Behavior: Replication of the Constraint Theory." *Justice Quarterly,* 2:89-98.

_____ (1986). *The Structure of Police Organizations.* New York: Praeger.

_____ (1989). "Do Stings Control Crime? An Evaluation of a Police Fencing Operation." *Justice Quarterly,* 6:27-45.

Mohr, L. (1973). "The Concept of Organizational Goal." *American Political Science Review,* 67:470-481.

Monkkenon, E. (1981). *Police in Urban America, 1860-1920.* Cambridge: Cambridge University Press.

Perrow, C. (1967). "A Framework for the Comparative Analysis of Organizations." *American Sociological Review,* 32:194-208.

_____ (1970). *Organizational Analysis: A Sociological View.* Monterey, CA: Brooks/Cole.

_____ (1979). *Complex Organizations: A Critical Essay,* 2nd ed. Glenview, IL: Scott, Foresman.

Roberg, R. (1979). *Police Management and Organizational Behavior: A Contingency Approach.* St. Paul, MN: West.

Sherman, L. (1980). "Causes of Police Behavior: The Current State of Quantitative Research." *Journal of Research in Crime and Delinquency,* 17:69-100.

Simon, H. (1964). "On the Concept of Organizational Goal." *Administrative Science Quarterly,* 9:1-22.

Slovak, J. (1986). *Styles of Urban Policing: Organization, Environment, and Police Styles in Selected American Cities.* New York: New York University Press.

Smith, D. & J. Klein (1983). "Police Agency Characteristics and Arrest Decisions." In G. Whitaker & C. Phillips (eds.) *Evaluating Performance of Criminal Justice Agencies,* pp. 63-97. Beverly Hills: Sage Publications.

Street, D., R. Vinter & C. Perrow (1966). *Organization for Treatment.* New York: Free Press.

Walker, S. (1977). *A Critical History of Police Reform.* Lexington, MA: Lexington.

Wilson, J. (1963). "The Police and Their Problems: A Theory." *Public Policy,* 12:189-216.

_____ (1968). *Varieties of Police Behavior: The Management of Law and Order in Eight Communities.* Cambridge: Harvard University Press.

Woodward, J. (1965). *Industrial Organization: Theory and Practice.* London: Oxford University Press.

7

Selection and Testing

Larry K. Gaines
Eastern Kentucky University

Victor E. Kappeler
Central Missouri State University

INTRODUCTION

The personnel selection process is one of the most important administrative functions in a police department. It is the process through which the
agency is rejuvenated by importing vital new human resources. Since officers often have complete careers with one agency, if the initial selection
decision is poorly made, the department is faced with retaining an inferior
officer for 20 years or more. Thus, selection decisions have long-term,
momentous implications for a department. No matter how well a department
is organized or administered, if the police officers who must perform daily
police responsibilities are not of the highest caliber, the department will not
reach its full potential in terms of maintaining order, reducing crime, and
providing important services to the community.

One of the factors which causes the selection process to be so critical is
organizational membership permanence created through civil service and
merit regulations. Once an officer has achieved civil service status, which is
usually after one year, the officer can be discharged only through disci-
plinary action. Officers in most agencies are afforded protections which
allow only the most indolent or criminal to be discharged. Thus, departments often are forced to retain marginal employees who never commit
serious infractions but who are never really productive.

Schultz (1984) maintains that organizations could save significant amounts of fiscal resources annually through more judicious selection procedures. His point is well taken. When an employee who is not capable of performing at the desired level is hired, it costs the organization in one or both of two ways: additional personnel costs to bring the organization up to the desired level; or the organization not fulfilling its mission when tasks are not completed or completed at an unacceptable level. With respect to police organizations, unqualified selections ultimately increase a department's risk of civil liability and cause it to provide services at an unsatisfactory level.

AN OVERVIEW OF POLICE SELECTION

The selection process is implemented in conjunction with the recruitment process. That is, the effectiveness or success which a department has in selecting officers is, to a great degree, dependent upon the recruitment process to acquire qualified applicants for the applicant pool. Wallace, Crandall, and Fay (1982:219) have identified the phases associated with the recruitment and selection processes:

(1) specify appropriate labor markets,

(2) seek out and attract qualified applicants,

(3) present the department in an attractive light as a potential employer,

(4) decide on criteria by which to accept and reject applicants,

(5) gather job information dictated by the selection criteria, and

(6) make the selection decision.

With the passage of the 1964 Civil Rights Act, identifying appropriate labor markets and seeking qualified applicants have become more critical in police selection. Litigation and the threat of litigation have caused a great deal of consternation as many departments lost lawsuits and were forced to pay large settlements, had race and sex hiring and promotion quotas imposed upon them, or both. Recruitment for many jurisdictions has become market-oriented as departments attempt to ensure appropriate race and sex representation in their hiring practices.

Discrimination and fair employment issues have perplexed many police administrators as they have attempted to balance female and minority representation on the department with hiring the "best qualified applicant." Typically, the minorities who apply for police positions do not score as well as their majority counterparts on a number of police screening devices (Gaines, Costello & Crabtree, 1989; Sproule, 1984; Winters, 1989), and personnel administrators frequently must make scoring adjustments to achieve selection parity or face possible discrimination litigation.

Once selection criteria are identified, the preferred philosophy of police selection is to screen-in applicants as opposed to screening-out applicants. Screening-in applicants denotes a process through which only the best of the qualified applicants are considered for employment. Screening-out applicants, by contrast, involves removing all unqualified applicants from the applicant pool and then considering for employment anyone who is at least minimally qualified—those who are not screened out. Obviously, police administrators want to select the best possible candidates. The difficulty comes in establishing a screening-in process that meets legal mandates and accomplishes affirmative action objectives.

LEGAL FRAMEWORK
OF POLICE SELECTION AND TESTING

In order to understand the issues and problems involved in police selection it is necessary to consider the legal framework which dictates employment practices. Legal restrictions on employment standards and tests are based on federal anti-discrimination law. This law is derived from a number of sources including court decisions, legislative enactments and governmental directives. Restrictions and requirements based on anti-discrimination law limit the standards and tests used to select police officers. At the same time, this law promotes fairness in employment and helps to ensure the use of objective selection procedures by police organizations.

The focal point of any discussion of the legality of an employment practice is the Civil Rights Act of 1964. This Act represents Congressional resolve to prohibit discriminatory practices. The Act defines discrimination as drawing distinctions from which to make decisions based on considerations of race, color, sex, national origin, or religion. Title VII of the Act affords broad and extensive protection, and its provisions against discrimination in employment apply to most employers and employees, including police departments. This legislation has proven to be a fertile source of litigation involving employment standards and testing. Since the adoption of the legislation and its amendment in 1972, a substantial body of case law has been generated by the federal courts.

The legislation has two unique aspects. First, it provides protection from discrimination for persons falling into certain classifications. Persons falling within these categories are afforded protection from discriminatory employment decisions that adversely affect them as individuals. Therefore, employers cannot discriminate against individuals based on their race, color, sex, national origin, or religion. Second, the legislation prohibits certain employers from engaging in practices that discriminate against these protected classes as groups. Hence, employers cannot use selection tests or standards that tend to discriminate against protected classes.

In *McDonnell Douglas v. Green* (1973) the Court developed legal procedures on how employment discrimination cases are to be litigated. The Court established that in discrimination cases the plaintiff-applicant has the initial burden of demonstrating discrimination. In order to satisfy this burden, plaintiffs must show:

(1) they belong to a protected class as defined by Title VII of the Civil Rights Act of 1964;

(2) they applied for a position that they were qualified to hold;

(3) they were rejected for the position; and

(4) following their rejection the employer continued to seek applicants with similar qualifications.

If these four requirements are met, the plaintiff has demonstrated a prima facie case of individual discrimination. This method of demonstrating discrimination is referred to as the *disparate treatment* method.

Showing that the employer's selection standard or test has an adverse impact on a protected class of individuals collectively is referred to as the *disparate impact* method. Disparate impact can be demonstrated in a number of ways, but generally the courts rely on statistical data indicative of a disparate rejection rate of minority candidates. In the past, the courts have accepted what has commonly been referred to as the four-fifths rule. Here the acceptance rate for minorities must be at least four-fifths or 80 percent of the acceptance rate for majority candidates. For example, if 60 percent of the white applicants are selected, then 48 percent of the minority applicants must be selected to avoid disparate impact discrimination.

A second disparate impact method that courts have relied upon consists of population comparisons of the racial composition of the agency relative to the racial composition of the community. For example, if a police department's personnel are 10 percent minority while the community contains a 45 percent minority population, the court may deem that disparate impact in selection has occurred. In the past, practices that tended to exclude minority candidates to a greater extent than their non-minority counterparts were usually held to be discriminatory. Recently, however, the court in *Wards Cove Packing Co. v. Antonia et al.* (1989) substantially increased the plaintiff's requirements regarding the disparate impact doctrine and significantly diminished employers' burden of proof by noting that statistical studies may be refuted by considering the labor market. The court also noted that plaintiffs could refute any labor market information and data. *Wards Cove*, essentially, is the climax of several cases where the court has rejected quotas or any attack which appears to be based on quotas.

After a plaintiff meets the burden of demonstrating discrimination, the burden of refuting the claim shifts to the employer. As a defense to a claim of discrimination, the Supreme Court has ruled that when an employment practice has been demonstrated to have an adverse impact on a protected class, the practice may only be justified by an illustration of "business necessity." The principles of adverse impact and business necessity were defined in the landmark Supreme Court decision of *Griggs v. Duke Power Company* (1971). This case established several principles of law that guide employment practices and the litigation of discrimination cases. The court held that selection tests that appear to be neutral cannot be used if they tend to "freeze" the status quo of discrimination. Therefore, tests which exclude minorities but cannot be shown to be related to job performance are prohibited. The Court went on to reason, however, that tests which are professionally developed, job-related and measure an applicant's job ability are permissible under Title VII of the Civil Rights Act of 1964. This means that if an employment practice operates to exclude members of a protected class, but can be shown to be related to job performance, it is permissible. This requires that a balancing test must occur to determine if an employment practice violates the provisions of the Civil Rights Act. Under such a test, the employer is required to show that the employment practice bears "a manifest relationship" to the job actually performed (Carter, Sapp & Stephens, 1989). If this cannot be demonstrated the practice is prohibited and the employer has failed to overcome the assumption of discrimination.

The protections granted by Title VII are not without exception, however. Title VII does not prohibit the use of subjective tests and the use of these tests alone does not render an entire selection process per se discriminatory. Because Title VII prohibits discrimination rather than simple arbitrariness or capriciousness, the mere existence of vague and subjective criteria alone is not sufficient proof of unlawful discrimination (*Lilly v. Harris-Teeter Supermarket,* 1983). The courts, however, view subjective standards and tests with a judicial jaundice. Still, disparate treatment or disparate impact must be established for a plaintiff to succeed in a Title VII action against an employer.

Similarly, Title VII of the Civil Rights Act of 1964 (as amended in 1972) has exceptions to the terms "employer" and "employee." Many cases indicate that select criminal justice employees are not covered by the provisions of the Act (Kappeler & del Carmen, 1989). A specific exemption to the legislation applies to elected public officials and their "personal staffs." Overall, federal court decisions on this exception provision have limited Title VII applicability for a variety of criminal justice personnel, including many deputy sheriffs, assistant district attorneys, and probation officers who are not covered by civil service. Therefore, these persons are not granted the protections of Title VII, although they may seek redress under another Civil Rights Act—42 U.S.C. Section 1983.

PRE-EMPLOYMENT STANDARDS

For purposes of police selection it is important to distinguish between standards and tests. Standards refer to criteria or qualifications necessary for an applicant to hold a position. They are usually rigid and require applicants to meet specified qualifications before they become eligible for employment with the agency. While selection standards may be based on tests, they are unlike tests in that they establish certain finite qualifications necessary to be considered for a police position.

Police employment standards vary from department to department, but may include requirements relating to vision, hearing, age, height, weight, biographical characteristics, educational levels, residency, and the absence of a history of drug use. Police organizations can choose among these and other standards so long as they are permissible within the legal framework of anti-discrimination law. In the following sections select police employment standards are considered. While the list is not comprehensive, it addresses several standards adopted by police organizations that have raised much debate from police administrators and scholars alike.

Vision Standards

Most police organizations have standards relating to an applicant's vision. While these standards vary from organization to organization, there is general agreement among police administrators that there should be a vision standard for police applicants (Holden, 1984; Cox, Crabtree, Joslin & Millett, 1987; Holden & Gemmeltoft, 1991). Numerous administrators feel that 20/20 uncorrected visual acuity is the only acceptable selection standard for police work (Holden, 1984), while others have requirements such as 20/45 uncorrected vision. The adoption of stringent vision standards is based on two rationales (Cox et al., 1987). First, glasses or contact lenses may become dislodged in the performance of critical police functions. While this possibility could result in a potentially fatal situation, especially in cases of deadly force, research shows that the dislodgment concern is mitigated by its infrequency. The second argument in support of a stringent uncorrected vision standard is based on the "optical blurring" argument. Proponents of a strict vision standard argue that impaired vision beyond 20/45 can hinder an officer's ability to recognize potential threats or identify suspects at distances. This argument has limited application as well since the identification of criminal suspects at great distances is improbable even with excellent vision.

While there are few studies of the vision standard, research indicates that such standards are usually developed and adopted by police organizations in an arbitrary fashion. Often these standards have little to do with police performance or research on the ability of police officers with vision problems to perform their jobs. This fact raises serious questions about the legal defensibility of the rigid uncorrected visual acuity standards.

One of the first cases decided by the courts on the issue of a police vision standard was *Toonen v. Brown County* (1985). In this case, the plaintiff filed action against the sheriff's department alleging discrimination. Toonen had applied for employment with the Brown County, Wisconsin Sheriff's Department, but was rejected for the position of deputy sheriff based on the department's vision standard. It was argued by Toonen that his poor vision was a handicap and that the vision standard was discriminatory because it was not sufficiently job-related. He argued, in part, that the vision standard was not job-related because the sheriff's department did not require its personnel to continue to meet the standard throughout their careers. Although the state appellate court found for the department and its standard, the case proceeded through the entire state court system until the Wisconsin Supreme Court reversed the appellate court's decision. Based on the Supreme Court's reversal, Toonen was subsequently hired as a deputy sheriff and given seniority and back pay. Although the vision standard issue has yet to be decided in the federal courts, this case poses problems for police departments that adopt rigid vision requirements.

Educational Standards

An ongoing debate in police selection is the use of a higher education standard for law enforcement officers (Carter, Sapp & Stephens, 1988). Proponents of the standard argue that college-educated police officers enhance the quality of law enforcement service to the community. Others argue that such requirements are not necessary because police officers with college educations do not perform better than their non-college-educated counterparts, education requirements may have an adverse effect on minorities, and college-educated police officers become bored and expect special treatment from their organizations (O'Rourke, 1971).

Administrators are free to adopt educational standards for police officer positions so long as the standards can be shown to be job-related. Historically, the courts have taken a dim view of adopting educational standards for blue-collar employment positions, but have supported educational requirements for professions. A decision by the United States Fifth Circuit Court of Appeals may make higher educational standards a reality for the police profession. In *Davis v. Dallas* (1985) the court addressed a 60-hour college education standard required by the Dallas Police Department. It was argued that the requirement had an adverse impact on minority applicants. The court, however, distinguished the police profession from other vocational positions and found that the education requirement bore a manifest relationship to the position of police officer. The court upheld the depart-ment's education standard reasoning that the relationship between the position and the education requirement mitigated any discriminatory effects.

Drug Use Standards

Drug use has become a concern of many Americans. This concern is evidenced by intense media attention and a vigorous push for mandatory drug testing in many employment settings. Police are not insulated from this movement to eradicate drug use in the workplace. Several studies conducted on police drug use indicate that police are as susceptible to drug abuse as citizens from other walks of life. Recognizing the potential for drug abuse and its serious consequences to law enforcement, police administrators are adopting employment standards requiring applicants to be relatively free of drug abuse histories. In fact, some preliminary research indicates that pre-employment use of illegal drugs is one of the best indicators of post-employment drug use by police officers (Kraska & Kappeler, 1988).

Adopting a drug-free history standard as a requirement of police employment does have legal consequences. In fact, the standard has been challenged in the federal courts (*Davis v. Dallas,* 1985). Civil action was brought against the Dallas Police Department claiming that a standard requiring police applicants not to have recent or excessive histories of mar-ijuana use had a disparate impact on minority applicants. Although the standard may have had a disparate impact on certain applicants, the court held the standard to be job-related and therefore permissible. The court rea-soned that "in light of the responsibility and discretion inherent in the posi-tion of police officer, as well as the compelling interest in enforcing existent criminal laws" it would uphold the department's pre-employment standard (p. 225). It is important to note, however, that the Dallas Police Department relied on an objective system from which to make employment decisions. The department developed a chart from which to consider the extent and frequency of past and current drug use by the applicant in selec-tion decision-making. This objective criterion may have insulated the department from an adverse court ruling.

Similarly, in *Shield Club v. City of Cleveland* (1986) police cadets brought civil action against the City of Cleveland, based on the police department's policy of denying final appointment of police cadets who were users of controlled drugs. It was argued that drug testing had an adverse effect on minority police cadets in their attempt to secure employment as police offi-cers. The federal District Court held that the department's policy of medi-cally-based drug testing and the rejection of applicants who tested positive for narcotics, amphetamines or hallucinogenics was job-related and not dis-criminatory. Again, the department under study relied on an objective test-ing method that prevented any form of individual discrimination. It seems that the lower federal courts, at least, are willing to accept drug-free history as a job-related standard for positions in law enforcement, if that standard is applied objectively and to all police candidates.

Physical Agility Standards

Police administrators have long extolled the virtues of employing physically capable police officers. The forerunner of physical agility standards were height-weight standards that were typically placed at levels which allowed only the tallest and largest of applicants to be hired. It was believed that police work was physically demanding, presented numerous bodily threats, and required officers who could, as a result of their size, control and subdue suspects. As of the 1960s, some police departments had minimum height requirements of six feet.

These minimum height requirements had an adverse impact on female and Hispanic applicants. For example, in *Vanguard Justice Society v. Hughes* (1979) the court noted that the Baltimore Police Department's height requirement of 5'7", which excluded 95 percent of the female population and only 32 percent of the male population, was *prima facie* evidence of sex discrimination. In *Mieth v. Dollard* (1976:1169) the court noted:

> The 5'9", 160-pound height and weight requirements set by the Alabama Department of Public Safety for the job of state trooper were not rationally related to achievement of any legitimate state interest . . . Contentions that exclusion of women from employment as state trooper[s] [was] intended for their protection and for the protection of the public was not sufficient to justify minimum height and weight limitations, which has the effect of excluding all women, since not only do women not need protectors but there was no record evidence that a woman could not perform the duties of a patrol officer . . . Evidence failed to establish . . . that tall officers hold advantage over smaller colleagues in effectuating arrests and administering emergency aid; furthermore, [the] contention that tall officers have a psychological advantage was not, as measure of job performance, sufficient constitutional justification for blanket exclusion of all individuals under specified height.

As a result of the numerous court decisions which consistently struck down police height requirements, many agencies developed physical agility tests in order to evaluate applicants' physical ability to perform police duties. The courts' reactions to these standards have been mixed. For example, in *Thomas v. City of Evanston* (1985) the court invalidated the city's physical agility test which included a half-mile run, stair climb, and an obstacle course because it discriminated against female applicants. In *United States v. Wichita Falls* (1988) the court upheld the Wichita Falls, Texas testing procedure where applicants were screened using an agility test which was less strenuous than one which was administered in the training academy after a sufficient training period. In *Eison v. Knoxville* (1983) the court upheld the dismissal of a female trainee who failed to pass the department's physical agility test during the training academy.

The Court, in *Thomas,* identified three conditions which physical agility tests must meet in order to be acceptable. First, any test must be based on a proper job analysis to determine the required work behaviors for successful performance of the job. Second, the test must represent the content of the job. Third, the test must be scored to discern those who are able to perform the job versus those who cannot. This third point is the most difficult since it is virtually impossible to identify at what point an individual's physical condition will detract from successful performance of the job, especially since most police agencies do not require officers to remain physically fit once they are employed. There are substantial numbers of veteran officers who cannot successfully complete their departments' entry-level physical agility tests.

Entry-level physical testing is moving toward health or normative testing rather than specific standards based on job requirements. That is, cut-off scores or norms are being established relative to the general population. A number of departments examine applicants'

(1) cardiovascular capacity,

(2) body fat composition,

(3) flexibility, and

(4) dynamic and absolute strength (Schofield, 1989).

Tests are developed to measure these attributes, and passing cut-off scores are established relative to population norms. Generally, it is assumed that police applicants should be at the 50th percentile in their age and sex groups in order to qualify for employment as police officers (see *United States v. Wichita Falls*).

Background and Work History

Police departments generally conduct an extensive investigation into an applicant's work history and behavior. These investigations are conducted as background investigations and polygraph examinations. Generally, the polygraph examination is an attempt to identify negative behavior such as illicit drug use and criminality while the background investigation attempts to investigate the applicant's social and employment histories. Many of the standards used in determining applicants' fitness for employment are some-what subjective and their content varies from one department to another.

It is not clear how past behaviors relate to future job performance as a police officer, as few validity studies have been conducted and their find-ings have been somewhat inconsistent (see Levy, 1967; Cohen & Chaiken, 1972). The courts have often struck down employment standards when there was adverse impact and the standards could not be shown to be job related. However, research seems to indicate that biographical information has potential in selecting police officers and future validity studies may uncover biographical traits which accurately predict future police perfor-mance (Malouff & Schutte, 1986).

In some instances, the background standards used by police to screen applicants have discriminated against minorities. As a result of social, eco-nomic, and cultural conditions and differences, minorities are more likely to have been involved in minor criminal behavior and to have had less employment success. If an employment standard discriminates against minorities and the standard is not job related (business necessity), the courts will disallow the standard.

Psychological Standards

The courts have held police departments liable when officers were not properly screened for psychological problems and later caused physical or emotional harm to citizens as a result of psychological problems (*Hild v. Bruner,* 1980; *Bonsignore v. City of New York,* 1981). Many departments retain the services of a licensed psychologist or psychiatrist. Standards used to screen out applicants are "professional" psychological standards in that they are determined by the psychologist as a result of professional expertise.

There is considerable controversy surrounding psychological tests. Research has shown that some psychological screening devices are racially biased (Winters, 1989), and the courts have recognized this fact (*League of United Latin American Citizens v. City of Santa Ana,* 1976). Problems have arisen when the psychologist has depended excessively upon one screening device, particularly a written test, or when adjustments are not made for specific items or groups of items which are known to have adverse effects on minorities.

Clearly, the most effective psychological screening includes multiple written and clinical evaluations of candidates. Multiple tests, using written tests supplemented with clinical evaluations, allow the psychologist to develop a complete profile of the candidate and therefore ultimately make a better decision relative to the candidate's suitability for police work. But even with multiple testing, the results are not always clear. Psychologists often develop rating schemes for classifying candidates which include acceptable, unacceptable, and uncertain. Here, the psychologists are unwilling to assume liability for those candidates who do not clearly show unacceptable tendencies. The police administrator, however, has no choice and should not accept any candidates unless the psychologist has rated them acceptable. The need to protect the public is too great to not abide by this policy.

PRE-EMPLOYMENT TESTING

Whereas pre-employment standards use cut-off scores and are administered on a pass-fail basis, tests tend to be used to rank candidates. Thus, a test creates a situation in which candidates compete against each other rather than against some pre-established standard. The two most commonly used tests in police selection are the written test and the oral interview board.

Written Tests

Prior to the 1964 Civil Rights Act and the numerous subsequent court decisions interpreting the Act, police departments primarily used intelligence tests or jurisdictionally specific knowledge tests to screen applicants. It was reasoned that more intelligent applicants would make better police officers and that jurisdictional knowledge tests would assist in hiring hometown applicants. Few efforts were made to determine if these domains actually had any impact on the applicant's ability to be a successful police officer, however.

Title VII of the 1964 Civil Rights Act required departments to establish the job-relatedness of their tests when there was adverse impact upon a protected class and when a discrimination suit was filed against the department. The courts, in numerous instances, disallowed the written test, and where discrimination had existed historically, imposed hiring and promotion quotas for minorities (see for example, *Johnson v. City of Albany, Georgia,* 1976).

It has been virtually impossible to develop written tests which predict which candidates will be "good" police officers. There are two reasons for this situation. First, there is little agreement within police circles as to what constitutes a good police officer, and even if there was agreement, a sufficiently sensitive written test to measure these traits probably would not be available. Second, since police departments screen out the unqualified or poor applicants, predictive validity studies are rarely feasible since the remaining officers are not representative of the potential selection population. That is, when validity studies are performed, they include only those applicants who scored higher on the entry-level screening tests and standards, and thus fall prey to the restricted range statistical problem (but for an example of a predictive validity study, see Gruber, 1986).

Minorities generally score lower on tests of cognitive skills. For example, Sproule (1984) and Gaines et al. (1989) found minorities to score on the average at least one standard deviation below their majority counterparts on police entry examinations. This frequently creates adverse impact, especially when the tests are used to rank the applicants.

Ranking applicants using written tests should be discouraged when adverse impact occurs. Written tests are power tests and as such are not related to any job standards or behavior; they are useful only in comparing candidates with each other (adequate predictive validity normally does not exist). Secondly, the actual distance between candidates represented by numerical test scores is not known. For example, in *Guardian Association of the New York City Police Department v. Civil Service Commission of the City of New York* the Court found that a 100-item test failed to adequately distinguish the candidates to justify rank-ordering. Half of the 36,797 applicants scored 91 or higher on the test and 2,000 applicants had scores of 94 to 97. As the number of candidates in the selection pool increases, the mathematical distance separating the candidates diminishes to the point that several candidates may be separated by less than one point. In the above example, it is doubtful that the performance of a candidate who scores 91 will be distinguishable from one who scored 94, and the use of such insignificant mathematical distinctions cannot be justified when discrimination occurs.

Third, all tests have some level of measurement error which would negate some of the differences among the scores. For example, even if a test had a reliability quotient of .90 (which is quite high for police selection tests), 19 percent of the variance associated with the test would be measurement error. Since in most cases police selection test scores are generally clustered very tightly, at least some of the rankings would be attributable to measurement error rather than candidates' actual abilities.

Giving deference to the problems with police written tests, there is movement to use interpretive methods other than ranking when using written tests. Gaines et al. (1989), Sproule (1984), and Moore (1983) have examined and compared the relative merits of ranking, grouping, and statistical adjustments of scores. Each of these schemes has advantages and disadvantages. However, the police administrator should almost always use grouping or statistical adjustments when interpreting written tests to avoid adverse impact.

The Oral Interview Board

The oral interview board is usually the capstone to the selection process. It is a process where police officials have an opportunity to review all the information collected during the selection process and directly observe and question the candidates. Inconsistencies and uncertainties can be clarified, and candidates can be evaluated first-hand in terms of their suitability for the department. Generally, the oral interview is the final ranking process which determines the order of selection.

Gaines and Lewis (1982) have identified a number of reliability and validity problems associated with the oral interview board. They found that reliability coefficients, although statistically significant, were not entirely adequate considering that scores are usually grouped together very tightly (as with written tests, measurement error plays a significant role in the actual rankings). They also identified several validity problems which in all probability would be fatal should discrimination litigation occur.

In a similar study, Falkenberg, Gaines, and Cox (1990) found a number of potential discrimination problems with the oral interview board. They examined a number of factors in an attempt to establish concurrent validity. None of the factors had sufficiently high correlations with board scores. Secondly, they found that female raters tended to discriminate against minority candidates. Since this research examined only one board, the results are not conclusive; however, it does point to a need for in-depth validity research into police oral interview boards.

Generally, oral interview boards consist of a board of raters who question each applicant using standardized questions and rate the applicants on several pre-established dimensions. The problem is that the rating task becomes too complex for the raters to accurately complete—raters must evaluate numerous responses in terms of accuracy and appropriateness, place numerical weights on the responses, and classify the responses onto the dimensions. This process may sound rather simplistic and straightforward. However, as the number of applicants increases, information processing becomes much more complex and difficult.

There are several procedures which can be implemented to improve the reliability and validity of the oral interview board. First, the number of rating dimensions should be minimal. Typically, raters evaluate candidates using from five to ten dimensions. However, the maximum number of dimensions should be no more than five to reduce the amount of rater information processing and decision-making. Second, the raters should be trained so that they clearly understand the process and how responses should be graded. Third, the rating scales should use behavioral anchors (as opposed to numerical or adjective scales) so that raters will have standards to compare with candidate responses. Finally, great care should be taken when selecting the rating dimensions. They should be clearly understood by the raters and amenable to measurement. For example, appearance is a common dimension, but it usually has little utility since all applicants normally dress appropriately and raters have difficulty in distinguishing among them. Dimensions such as acceptability or "knowledge for the position" are inappropriate because they are too general and difficult to understand and evaluate in terms of behavior or responses. Overall or global dimensions should not be used as they tend to confuse the rating process. Dimensions should be critical components of the job and should be clear and meaningful to the raters. Every attempt should be made to simplify the process and develop standards, dimensions, and questions which allow for effortless and obvious measurement.

SUMMARY

The selection process is a critical component of police personnel administration. Selection decisions are the foundation of any department's future, and as such, departments should spare no expense or effort in selecting their personnel. Great care should be taken to develop a system which not only attempts to select the best-qualified applicants, but also addresses affirmative action concerns. When establishing selection standards, due consideration should be given to the labor market. Police managers want to select the best applicants, but at the same time, do not want to reduce the potential applicant pool through restrictive standards to the point that the department cannot acquire necessary personnel. Selection should be considered a balancing act in which numerous problems and forces are constantly weighed and considered.

REFERENCES

Bonsignore v. City of New York, 521 F. Supp. 394 (1981).

Carter, D.L., A.D. Sapp & D.W. Stephens (1989). "Higher Education as a Bona Fide Occupational Qualification (BFOQ) for Police: A Blueprint." *American Journal of Police*, 7,2:1-28.

_____ (1988). *The State of Police Education: Policy Direction for the 21st Century*. Washington, DC: Police Executive Research Forum.

Cohen, R. & J. Chaiken (1972). *Police Background Characteristics and Performance: Summary Report* (No. R-999-DDJ). New York: Rand Institute.

Cox, T.C., A. Crabtree, D. Joslin & A. Millett (1987). "A Theoretical Examination of Police Entry-Level Uncorrected Visual Standards." *American Journal of Criminal Justice*, 11,2:199-208.

Davis v. Dallas, 777 F.2d 205 (5th Cir. 1985), *cert. denied*, 106 S. Ct. 1972 (1986).

Eison v. Knoxville, 570 F. Supp. 11 (1983).

Forrester v. White, 56 U.S.L.W. 4069 (1988).

Falkenberg, S., L.K. Gaines & T.C. Cox (1990). "The Oral Interview Board: What Does it Measure?" *Journal of Police Science and Administration,* 17,1:32-39.

Gaines, L.K., P. Costello & A. Crabtree (1989). "Police Selection Testing: Balancing Legal Requirements and Employer Needs." *American Journal of Police,* 8,1:137-152.

Gaines, L.K. & B.R. Lewis (1982). "Reliability and Validity of the Oral Interview Board in Police Promotions: A Research Note." *Journal of Criminal Justice,* 10:63-79.

Good, G.W. & A.R. Augsburger (1987). "Uncorrected Visual Acuity Standards for Police Applicants." *Journal of Police Science and Administration,* 15,1:18-23.

Griggs v. Duke Power Company, 401 U.S. 424 (1971).

Gruber, G. (1986). "The Police Applicant Test: A Predictive Validity Study." *Journal of Police Science and Administration,* 14,2:121-129.

Guardian Association of the New York City Police Department, Inc. v. Civil Service Commission of the City of New York et al. (1980) 630 F.2d 79 (2d Cir. 1980), *cert. denied,* 452 U.S. 940 (1981).

Hild v. Bruner, 496 F. Supp. 93 (1980).

Holden, R.N. (1984). "Vision Standards for Law Enforcement: A Descriptive Study." *Journal of Police Science and Administration* 12,2:125-129.

_____ & L.L. Gemmeltoft (1991). "*Toonen v. Brown County*: The Legality of Police Vision Standards." *American Journal of Police,* 10,1.

Johnson v. City of Albany, Georgia, 413 F. Supp. 782 (1976).

Kappeler, V.E. & R.V. del Carmen (1989). "The Personal Staff Exemption to Title VII of the Civil Rights Act of 1964: May Some Criminal Justice Personnel be Dismissed at Will?" *Criminal Law Bulletin,* 25,4:340-361.

Kraska, P.B. & V.E. Kappeler (1988). "Police On-Duty Drug Use: A Theoretical and Descriptive Examination." *American Journal of Police,* 7,1:1-28.

League of United Latin American Citizens v. City of Santa Ana, 410 F. Supp. 873 (1976).

Levy, R.J. (1967). "Predicting Police Failures." *Journal of Criminal Law, Criminology, and Police Science,* 58:265-276.

Lilly v. Harris-Teeter Supermarket, 720 F.2d 326, 338 (4th Cir. 1983).

Malouff, J.M. & N.S. Schutte (1986). "Using Biographical Information to Hire the Best New Police Officers: Research Findings." *Journal of Police Science and Administration,* 14,3:175-177.

McDonnell Douglas v. Green, 411 U.S. 972 (1973).

Mieth v. Dollard, 418 F. Supp. 1169 (1976).

Moore, R. (1983) "Strategies for Increasing the Number of Black Police Executives." *FBI Law Enforcement Bulletin,* (May):19-25 and (June):15-21.

O'Rourke, W.J. (1978). "Should All Policemen be College Trained?" *The Police Chief,* 43,7:36.

Schofield, D.L. (1989). "Establishing Health and Fitness Standards: Legal Considerations." *FBI Law Enforcement Bulletin,* (June):25-31.

Schultz, C. (1984). "Saving Millions Through Judicious Selection." *Public Personnel Management Journal,* 13,4:409-415.

Shield Club v. City of Cleveland, 647 F. Supp. 274 (N.D. Ohio 1986).

Sproule, C.F. (1984). "Should Personnel Selection Tests be Used on a Pass-Fail, Grouping, or Ranking Basis?" *Public Personnel Management Journal,* 13,4:375-394.

Thomas v. City of Evanston, 610 F. Supp. 422 (C.D. Ill. 1985).

United States v. Wichita Falls, 47 F.E.P. 1629 (N.D. Tex. 1988).

Vanguard Justice Society v. Hughes, 471 F. Supp. 670 (1979).

Wallace, M.J., N.F. Crandall & C.H. Fay (1982). *Administering Human Resources.* New York: Random House.

Wards Cove Packing Co. v. Antonia, et al., ___ U.S. ___, 109 S. Ct. 2115 (1989).

Winters, C.A. (1989). "Psychology Tests, Suits, and Minority Applicants." *Police Journal,* 62,1:22-30.

8

Women In Policing[1]

Donna C. Hale
Shippensburg University

INTRODUCTION

The expansion of the Equal Employment Opportunity Act (EEOA) in 1972 to include public as well as private employers, permitted women to enter police patrol work. Prior to that time, women in policing performed primarily auxiliary (clerical and support) services and were assigned to work with children and women. Since 1972, however, policewomen have slowly integrated police departments.

By 1989, though, the percentage of female sworn police officers had still only reached 7.9 percent (United States Department of Justice, 1989:241).[2] This chapter examines why policewomen have experienced such slow integration into patrol work. A review of the literature on women in policing written over the past 65 years, but especially the research on women on patrol during the last 15 years, provides an explanation for their limited utilization. Based on this literature, recommendations for the future acceptance of women on patrol are made.

A useful framework which explains the role of women in police work and the problems women face in integrating police work is presented by Berg and Budnick (1986). They suggest three possibilities. First, they consider structural-functional theory which ascribes separate roles in society to men and women. Women are responsible for the home and children, while men are the providers and decisionmakers. Conflict theory proposes that men are the power-holders in society and women possess lower-status positions and are prohibited from the work force, unions, and education. Last is gender labeling, which posits that both men and women are socialized from birth to appropriate roles and activities.

Two of these three perspectives, structural-functionalism and gender labeling, are interwoven into this paper to explain how, over time, the policewoman's role has been perceived by peers, supervisors, and the public. These explanations illustrate that societal values are reflected in the position that women hold in police work. Conflict theory is given less emphasis in explaining the utilization of women in police work, however, because police work has traditionally been considered a low-status position. As useful as conflict theory may be for explaining blocked access for women into such fields as law and medicine, it does not seem quite as helpful in accounting for the experiences of women in policing.

A STRUCTURAL-FUNCTIONAL EXPLANATION

From the early 1900s until the expansion of the EEOA, and the creation of the Equal Employment Opportunity Commission to oversee its enforcement in 1972, policewomen were responsible for protection-prevention work with women and children, especially girls (Hamilton, 1925; Feinman, 1980; Vollmer, 1930; Linn & Price, 1985; Pogrebin, 1986). In fact, the newly appointed policewomen requested that cases involving women, girls, and children be assigned to them; they were willing to leave traffic, detective, and regular patrol duties to policemen (Harris, 1926). The EEOA, though, clearly marked the end of separate tasks for males and females in police work.

There is little doubt that early policewomen were assigned to handle children and their problems because of the female nurturing role (Hamilton, 1925; Feinman, 1980). This role coincided with societal values that made mothers responsible for insuring that children grew up to be good citizens (Lord, 1986). Furthermore, the early policewomen's movement (1910-1930) received support from both national womens' groups and prestigious civic and social hygiene associations.[3]

Examples from two California police departments illustrate the role of policewomen and reflect the organizational support that the policewoman's movement received. The Los Angeles Police Department created the City Mother's Bureau in October 1914 and hired policewomen to handle "cases of delinquent and pre-delinquent children whose parents desired informal intervention from a law enforcement agency but were reluctant to file a formal report against their children to the police" (Odem & Schlossman, 1991). The Bureau's work was primarily preventive and intended to preserve the moral welfare of girls and boys. Furthermore, Odem and Schlossman indicate that in Progressive-era Los Angeles, policewomen were appointed mainly to keep young women under public gaze during their leisure hours. Policewomen were used to monitor, investigate, and punish young girls whose behavior flouted social and sexual conventions. This role illustrates the influence of the social hygiene movement that was concerned about the spread of venereal diseases.

In 1925 August Vollmer opened the Crime Prevention Division in the Berkeley, California Police Department. This unit was headed by policewoman Elizabeth Lossing, a psychiatric social worker, who had previous therapeutic work experience with problem children. Vollmer hired Lossing to educate the Berkeley community about the dangers of not treating predelinquent behavior; and to identify and treat problem children (Liss & Schlossman, 1986).

The separate roles of policemen and policewomen were emphasized by the International Association of Chiefs of Police (IACP) at its meeting in 1922 where it was recommended that policewomen meet higher education and training standards than policemen. This training and education was to be in subjects related to women's professions: social work, nursing, and teaching. This requirement for women, and not for men, was justified on the grounds that women were responsible for protection-prevention work with women and children (Harris, 1926; Vollmer, 1930; Walker, 1977; and Feinman, 1980). At the same meeting, the IACP stated that policewomen were essential to police work and recommended that police departments establish separate women's units (Melchionne, 1974). The separation by gender and duties within the police department clearly reinforced that policewomen were responsible for the care of women and children (Walker, 1977), while men were assigned to conduct traditional patrol and detective functions. The Woman's Bureau was implemented within police departments and delegated jurisdiction over youth cases, some patrol of public places, detention of children and women (Pigeon, 1929), and supplementing "the work of the men's department, making the entire organization operate as a more perfect whole" (Hutzel, 1923:78). The purpose of policewomen was to aid and assist policemen "by seeking a quiet unassuming way to prevent crime." Effective police service was contingent on how well policewomen cooperated with the men (Hamilton, 1925:195).

Although policewomen were predominantly protection-prevention-oriented, they also were described as invaluable in preventing shoplifting in Washington, D.C. stores, more successful than male officers in investigating major crimes when it came to questioning the mistresses or confidants of professional criminals, and well-suited for interrogating female criminals (Brownlow, 1927). Their success in these areas was primarily attributed to their gender because:

(1) no one would suspect a woman working in retail to be other than a clerk; and

(2) female criminals and/or female associates of criminals could not use their "feminine charms" as successfully with female police officers as they could with male officers during interrogations.

The decline of the early policewomen's movement was attributed to the Great Depression, when jobs were primarily held by men as the providers for the family (Horne, 1979; Mishkin, 1981). From then until the extension of the EEOA in 1972, the role of women in police work was primarily auxiliary in nature—performing duties that aided and assisted policemen in conducting the duties of patrol.

GENDER LABELING

Gender labeling holds that individuals are socialized from birth to their respective roles in society. This not only affects individuals' own perceptions of what they can and cannot do, but also the perceptions of others regarding the roles of males and females in society.

Until women went on patrol in 1972, policewomen traditionally fulfilled roles that assisted and aided policemen. Therefore, there was little resistance to their role in police work until the time that they went on patrol. It was then that they encountered many newly created obstacles challenging their capabilities to perform what was perceived by both their peers and supervisors—as well as the public—as "men's work" (Milton, 1975; Johns, 1979; Homant, 1983; Lord, 1986; Balkin, 1988).

Clearly, policewomen on patrol have faced many obstacles from both their peers and management (Milton, 1978), who believe that they cannot perform patrol duties because they have neither the physical strength to do the job (Charles, 1982; Grennan, 1987); the authoritarian presence to handle violent confrontations (Morash, 1986; Grennan, 1987); nor the ability to serve as backup to their partners in high-pressure situations (LaBeff & Williams, 1982; Bryant, Dunkerley & Kelland, 1985). Attempts by supervisors to either overprotect policewomen (Milton, 1978; Martin, 1980; Remmington, 1983; Bryant et al., 1985; Lord, 1986), or keep them from areas with high violence (Vega & Silverman, 1982) further reinforce the view that women are not capable of performing patrol. One of the concerns which has caused stress for policewomen is an expressed fear, on the part of both wives and public officials, of sexual misconduct between policemen and policewomen (Milton, 1978; Taylor, 1974). This fear suppresses mentoring between the policewoman and her male peers and/or supervisors because, should mentoring occur, rumors of a sexual liaison arise (LaBeff & Williams, 1982; Morash, 1986; Wexler & Logan, 1983).

As a result of gender labeling, policewomen generally are viewed by management as less dedicated and are passed over for promotion because they are perceived as being less committed to a long-term career in law enforcement than men (Sherman, 1975). Management fears that they will leave policing to marry and have children (Bryant et al., 1985; Pogrebin, 1986). Interestingly, Fry (1983) studied the turnover rate in a sheriff's department and found that female officers resigned to accept positions in other law enforcement agencies because assignments (primarily custodial positions) and promotional opportunities were limited. He recommended that more innovative personnel policies be developed to retain women in the department.

Martin (1990), studying five departments for the period 1986-1988, found that the average non-retirement turnover rate for women was 5.3 percent compared to 3.2 percent for men. However, she indicates that the best predictor of women's turnover in an agency is the turnover rate for men, suggesting that department policies and local labor market decisions have similar effects on men's and women's decisions to leave policing. For women, Martin attributes the higher turnover rates and shorter police careers to several factors, including (1) an unrealistic view of police work at the time of hiring, and (2) rotating shifts and uncertain hours that are problematic for women with child-care responsibilities. She recommends that police departments consider the effects of rotating shifts, burnout, and abuses of leave on women's decisions to remain in policing.

Probably the most frequent stereotype of policewomen depicts them as neither emotionally, physically, nor psychologically able to handle police work—"a man's job" (Milton, 1975; Charles, 1982; Remmington, 1983; Jones, 1986). Bell (1982) indicated that male officers do not believe women can handle the danger and hazards of police work.

LaBeff and Williams (1982) found that although male officers believe that both male and female officers could communicate effectively on the job, they preferred women to be responsible for their traditional roles of clerical and maternal duties. This "left-handed compliment" reflects the traditional value system's support for the woman's role in assisting and aiding the male officer.

Weisheit (1987) points out that there is much discussion in the literature focusing on the males' resistance to policewomen, but almost no recognition of the concerns males have about the police organizational response to women. He suggests that there may be many male officers who are not so much concerned about the *performance* of policewomen as they are with what they see as the preferential treatment of females by the police organization.

The following section summarizes the work performance research regarding women on patrol. This literature clearly indicates that, initially, job performance was the focus of study due to the speculation regarding whether or not a woman could handle a "man's job."

WHAT THE RESEARCH SHOWS

The early patrol evaluation studies revealed that women performed patrol activities as well as men (Bloch, Anderson & Gervais, 1973; Bloch & Anderson, 1974; Sherman, 1975; Sichel, Friedman, Quint & Smith, 1978; Balkin, 1988). Balkin (1988) concluded that all the major evaluations found no important differences between policemen and policewomen, and that policewomen capably perform patrol duties.[4] Fry and Greenfield (1980) and Snortum and Beyers (1983) reached similar conclusions.

One area of particular concern was womens' handling of violent situations. The New York City evaluation (Sichel et al., 1978) indicated that female officers appeared more effective in handling potentially violent situations than their male counterparts, who were more likely to be the subjects of citizen complaints. Women and men were equally unlikely to use force or display a weapon (Balkin, 1988).

Grennan's (1987) analysis of 3,701 incidents taken from Firearms Discharge/Assault on Officer reports found no difference in the injury rates between male and female officers, no difference in the number of injuries to male or female partners in patrol teams during violent confrontations with citizens, and the male partner in male/female teams was more likely to discharge a firearm than the female partner. He concluded that female officers reacted the same as male officers to violent situations, and that female officers are more emotionally stable than male officers because they do not have to project the "macho" image that is part of the male personality (see also Horne, 1979). Instead of using physical force to confront criminals, policewomen use interpersonal skills (Weisheit, 1987; C. Martin, 1979).

In interviews with battered women who received police assistance, Kennedy and Homant (1983) learned that these victims perceived policewomen as more capable of calming men down, preventing violence, understanding the man, and improving the situation through discussion. It was the ability of policewomen to show concern (usually by providing information) that contributed to their superior rating by the battered women. The authors cautioned, however, that the different set of values and goals displayed by policewomen in domestic violence situations should not "be taken to imply that policemen are insensitive to battered women" (Homant & Kennedy, 1985).

After assessing eight major evaluations of female work performance on patrol,[5] Morash and Greene (1986) identified several shortcomings, including:

(1) a failure to measure the accomplishment of identifiable police tasks, or to specify proffered behavior;

(2) an emphasis on conformity to male stereotypes;

(3) methodological limitations—for example, the failure to obtain representative samples of police tasks and situations; and,

(4) an overemphasis on the violent and dangerous aspects of the police occupation.

Consequently, they conclude that generalizations from this body of literature are at best tenuous and misleading. Morash and Greene's findings concerning methodological limitations parallel earlier comments by Charles and Parsons (1978), who concluded that the studies on policewomen often employed small samples and short study periods and had results with limited applicability.

Similar to Homant and Kennedy's (1985) note about interpreting the way that men handle domestic violence, Morash and Greene indicate that just because women's styles of policing differ from men's, this should not be a reason to interpret them as undesirable. Instead, Morash and Greene (1986:247-249) argue that "perhaps such differences should set the standards against which men might be compared. Such a reversal in interpretation forces a thorough analysis of the police role."

Martin (1990) recommends that, because sex role stereotypes often create double standards of behavior, police departments should develop specific, job-related performance evaluation measures and periodically audit supervisory evaluations to address the inevitable inequities that occur in performance assessments. Golden (1981:31) points out that "performance and co-worker attitudes are closely linked in any occupational situation but especially in policing." Consequently, the roles that men and women are assigned within the organization lead to the development of stereotypes and the perpetuation of myths.

STEREOTYPES AND MYTHS
ABOUT WOMEN IN POLICING

As Morash and Greene (1986) noted, the major evaluation studies overemphasized the violent and dangerous aspects of police work. However, this emphasis also is shared by the public. The research on citizens' attitudes toward women in policing indicates that the public perceives police work as dangerous and thinks that only a man can handle the job.

Van Wormer (1981) listed possible advantages and disadvantages of using *men* on patrol. The advantages reflect both the stereotypes of men as the authority and power holders as well as gender labeling. Men are deemed best at having physical strength, adaptability to shift work, aggressiveness, and related job experience (i.e., military). The disadvantages of employing men included the misuse of authority and power (increased citizen complaints, poor public relations, and physical brutality), an unwillingness to share the power and security of law enforcement positions with women, and male overprotection of female partners. Policemen also have less formal education than women officers, have a poor reputation, and are insensitive when questioning rape victims.

These myths and stereotypes about the role of men in police work are reflected in the following section, which examines how the public evaluates the effectiveness of women on patrol. It is evident that police work is seen as confrontational and violent, and that women are perceived as not having the physical ability to deal with this type of work.

How the Public Perceives Female Police Officers

Studies that addressed the public's response to women on patrol found that the public's perception of the role of policing affected attitudes toward women on patrol. For example, Kerber, Andes, and Mittler (1977) found that the majority of the people interviewed accepted women in more expanded police roles and only viewed male officers as more competent in stopping a fist fight. Johns' (1979) study of undergraduate males and females in a criminal justice program concluded that the students viewed police work as a man's field and that women were not suited for the physical work of policing. Comparing law enforcement students' attitudes to those of police officers recorded in previous studies, Golden (1981) concluded that although college students expressed more favorable attitudes toward the utilization of women as patrol officers than did the male police officers cited in previous studies, students shared attitudes with the officers regarding the specific attributes of physical ability, strength, and emotional stability.

Another study by Sterling and Owen (1982:336-337) examined "whether it is the social role or the sex role that determines how demanding or reasoning behavior is perceived by others." Students were asked to evaluate audiotapes of both male and female police officers interacting with a student in a demanding or reasoning manner. The authors concluded that sex role was more important than social role in determining how assertive behavior is perceived. They found that both female and male students assigned male characteristics—tenacity, assertiveness, and activity—to the female police officers. While female officers acting assertively were considered less feminine, male officers could be reasoning or demanding, without having their masculinity questioned. Furthermore, the study found that challenging the female officer was more appropriate, and losing to her in the confrontation was more demeaning. Consequently, Sterling and Owen concluded that although female officers are "seen as having male characteristics, they are not considered as legitimate male officers" (1982:340).

The authors recommended that police departments convince the public that female police officers are "competent, sure of actions and not easily pushed around in verbal and/or physical confrontations" (1982:340).

These studies reveal that sex role stereotyping labels police work as both crime fighting and a masculine role (Kennedy & Homant, 1981; Homant, 1983). The conclusions of the Sterling and Owen study regarding the importance of sex roles support earlier comments by McGeorge and Wolfe (1976) that what female officers in their study perceived as public respect may have been attributable to citizens treating female officers differently because they were not "regular" police officers. That is, since women on patrol was a new phenomenon, the public initially behaved "traditionally" toward female officers by being deferent, polite, and respectful.

The Perceptions of Police Officers

Dorsey and Giacopassi (1986) measured differences in levels of cynicism between male and female officers. They found that both female and male officers perceived police work as authoritarian, inherently stressful, and dangerous. They concluded that male and female officers have similar patterns of cynicism, but found that the educated female officer is more cynical than her uneducated male counterparts.

Davis (1984) found policewomen significantly more authoritarian than policemen and more cynical about human motivation as it affects obedience to the law. He concluded that the predispositions of women to intervene when infractions were observed and their fewer arrests suggested that women may be more flexible than males in their approach to enforcement. Women did not experience any more general job-related stress, but perhaps due to the physical vulnerability of women, danger as a specific stressor was more important to policewomen than policemen. Although policewomen's self-confidence was significantly lower than males, they did perceive themselves as equally effective as their male counterparts.

Wexler and Quinn (1985) surveyed the perceived training needs of female and male candidates for sergeant positions in the San Francisco Police Department and found substantial similarities. However, the findings indicated that female officers had lower self-evaluations than their male counterparts—possibly attributed to women having less street and patrol experience and "a higher proportion of nonsupportive responses from co-workers" (1985:101). Consequently, the authors recommended that there should not be separate training, but that training should be "structured in such a way that it enhances the women's perceptions of their own competencies and helps increase the likelihood they achieve their goals" (1985:102). One way that this can be achieved is by training men and women together and training male co-workers "to recognize female competency and accept female leadership" (1985:102). This can be accomplished by exposing the men and women to training that utilizes credible women as trainers and training materials that portray women in supervisory as well as subordinate positions.

DISCUSSION

How do we address the obstacles that women encounter from both their peers and police management? A common thread in the literature is training focusing on physical training and self-defense (Milton, Abramowitz, Crites, Gates, Mintz & Sandler, 1974; Martin, 1979; Charles, 1981, 1982; Martin, 1990). Charles (1982) indicates that, although in general, women may not be as physically strong as men, through training women may attain a level of fitness well within the normal demands of the profession. Vega and Silverman (1982) recommend that future training emphasize role play responses to violent confrontations, teach methods of conflict resolution, and include physical and assertiveness training. Remmington (1983) recommends self-defense programs, and more rigorous supervision of backup officers in order to enable women to handle situations alone. This would, she believes, improve their self-image as well as bolster men's beliefs in policewomen's competence.

Martin (1990) presents promising evidence that police executives are "beginning to recognize the importance of departmental physical training programs (conditioning, diet, and stress reduction) for both male and female officers." She also found that the "salience of the physical differences issue has decreased because [policewomen] have proven their ability to defend themselves and their partners" (1990:xiii). Also, defensive tactics courses and departmental policies have curbed officers' physical aggressiveness.

Another area of training recommended at the police academy level is sensitivity training to modify the machismo aura of the police department. The presence of women in policing as academy instructors as well as including instructional material that describes equal employment opportunity, sexual harassment, and grievance procedures will enhance the opportunities for women entering police work (Martin, 1990).

Equally important to the successful integration of women into policing is the firm commitment of police leadership (Bouza, 1975). Bouza stressed that all police personnel must be provided an opportunity to succeed and that it must be acknowledged that males as well as females sometimes fail in the performance of their duties. Goldstein (1977:270) similarly emphasized that police administration is responsible for providing "clear evidence that members of minority groups . . . will have equal opportunities regarding assignments and promotions."

Warner, Steel and Lovrich (1989:562) have recently determined that success for women in policing is "highly dependent upon a formal administrative structure established specifically to achieve this goal." They found that the most important institutional factor associated with hiring of women was affirmative action programs with formal goals and guidelines. Further, those departments governed by court-enforced plans of action registered the greatest gains in utilization of women as police officers.

Martin (1990) concluded that "at the end of 1986 more than half of all large municipal agencies had affirmative action policies that contributed to the growing numbers of women in policing" (1990:xvi). However, police departments differed in "how vigorously these EEO policies have been publicized and how actively they have been enforced. In departments where top management [emphasized] that sexual harassment and discrimination [would] not be tolerated, women have spoken out about problems and seized on the opportunities available to them" (1990:xvii).

CONCLUSION

From the previous discussion of women in policing, it is clear that their role in police work has been defined both by the attitudes and values of society and by the police work environment. Initially, women were only responsible for protection-prevention work with women and children. Until 1972 policewomen continued to be limited to aiding and assisting policemen in their work.

The way that females as patrol officers are perceived by their male cohorts and supervisors has a tremendous impact on the performance of women in policing. It is clear that police work continues to be perceived as masculine (Milton, 1975; Dorsey & Giacopassi, 1986). Consequently, women who enter police work today still are faced with the perception that police work is inappropriate for them.

Why have women not made greater advancements in patrol work? From this review of the literature, it is readily apparent that policemen and policewomen are comparable in their performance, and that the public perceives them as equally effective, except in the handling of violent or confrontational situations. In these circumstances, the public perceives the policeman as more effective because of his physical attributes. The primary obstacle to women in policing is the attitudes of male officers (Milton, 1975; Horne, 1979; Johns & Barclay, 1979), as well as discrimination from within police departments (Bell, 1982). Sex role conceptions are a "severe obstacle to women seeking law enforcement careers" (Steffensmeier, 1979:41).

In the early policewomen's movement, societal values were mirrored in the police department by the separate roles and separate divisions for men and women in policing. Writing in the late 1980s, Balkin (1988) indicates that policemen do not like policewomen because of cultural values about sex roles and work. He believes that change in policemen's attitudes comes with changes in culture. Male officers' attitudes—not policewomens' performance—appear to be the main problem in introducing women into law enforcement (Golden, 1981). Resistance to women in policing is attributed to the social change process and the attitudes of both policemen and police management (Price & Gavin, 1982). For example, Bloch et al. (1973) found that black officers were more favorable towards policewomen than were white officers, and younger officers were more favorable to women than were older officers (see also Chandler, 1983). The opportunity structure of the police organization that limits promotion of women, and stereotypes that emphasize machismo, physical strength, and assertiveness are the major barriers to women in policing (Milton, 1978; Vega & Silverman, 1982; Remmington, 1983; Grennan, 1987).

Regarding future evaluation and research on women in policing, it is important to reiterate earlier observations about the weaknesses in design and analysis that limited previous studies. However, from past research we can develop an agenda for future analysis and action regarding the utilization of policewomen. For example, Martin (1990) recommends comparing the experiences of policewomen with the experiences of women entering other male-dominated occupations. She also suggests using detailed exit interviews of both male and female officers to aid the development of strategies for retaining female officers. It also will be important to identify those organizational responses to policewomen that policemen find most troublesome (Weisheit, 1987).

The barriers to women on patrol are not their inability or their incompetence but rather the traditional attitude that law enforcement is a man's job (Martin, 1980; Golden, 1981; Bell, 1982; Price, 1985; Lord, 1986; Balkin, 1988). By departments focusing on training to improve physical and psychological limitations and by sensitizing both peers and supervisors to the effectiveness of policewomen, progress can be made in facilitating the full integration of policewomen into every aspect of modern police work.

NOTES

1   The author wishes to thank Sean Grennan, Peter Horne, Merry Morash, and Barbara Raffel Price for their comments on an earlier draft of this paper. Of course, the author bears sole responsibility for any errors or oversights.

2　Melchionne (1974) estimated that by 1984 the percentage of women as sworn officers would increase by 10 to 15 percent. According to the *Uniform Crime Reports* (United States Department of Justice, 1984), the total percentage of sworn female officers in the United States for 1984 was 5.6 percent. Since 1984 the percentages as reported by the annual *Uniform Crime Reports* have been: 6.2 percent for 1985; 6.7 percent for 1986; 7.1 percent for 1987; 7.5 percent for 1988; and 7.9 percent for 1989.

3　These groups included the League of Women Voters, the General Federation of Women's Clubs, the American Social Hygiene Association, the National Young Women's Christian Association, the Woman's Christian Temperance Union, the Daughters of the American Revolution, the National Council of Women, and the Congress of Parents and Teachers (Owings, 1925; Pigeon, 1929; Melchionne, 1974).

4　These studies included the Pennsylvania State Police (1973); Dayton Police Department (Weldy, 1976); Illinois State Troopers (Ayoob, 1978); United States Air Force Security Police (Rutland, 1978); Los Angeles Police Department (Hickman, 1983); and El Monte (California) Police Department (Snortum & Beyers, 1983).

5　The studies assessed included the Pennsylvania State Police (1973); Washington, D.C. (Bloch & Anderson, 1974); St. Louis (Sherman, 1975); California (California Highway Patrol, 1976); Denver (Bartlett & Rosenblum, 1977); Newton, Massachusetts (Kizziah & Morris, 1977); New York City (Sichel et al., 1978); and Philadelphia (Bartell Associates, 1978).

REFERENCES

Ayoob, M. (1978). "Perspectives on Female Troopers." *Trooper,* 3:32-35, 99-101, 103.

Balkin, J. (1988). "Why Policemen Don't Like Policewomen." *Journal of Police Science and Administration,* 16,1:29-38.

Bartell Associates (1978). *The Study of Police Woman Competency in the Performance of Sector Police Work in the City of Philadelphia.* State College, PA: author.

Bartlett, H. & A. Rosenblum (1977). *Policewoman Effectiveness.* Denver, CO: Civil Service Commission and Denver Police Department.

Bell, D. (1982). "Policewomen: Myths and Reality." *Journal of Police Science and Administration* 10,1:112-120.

Berg, B. & K. Budnick (1986). "Defeminization of Women in Law Enforcement: A New Twist in the Traditional Police Personality." *Journal of Police Science and Administration,* 14,4:314-319.

Bloch, P., D. Anderson & P. Gervais (1973). *Policewomen on Patrol: Major Findings,* First Report, Vol. 1. Washington, DC: Police Foundation.

Bloch, P. & D. Anderson (1974). *Policewomen on Patrol: Final Report.* Washington, DC: Police Foundation.

Bouza, A. (1975). "Women in Policing." *FBI Law Enforcement Bulletin,* 44:2-7.

Brownlow, L. (1927). "The Policewoman and the Woman Criminal." *National Municipal Review:*467-468.

Bryant, L., D. Dunkerley & G. Kelland (1985). "One of the Boys?" *Policing,* 2,3:236-244.

California Highway Patrol (1976). *Women Traffic Officer Project.* Sacramento, CA: author.

Chandler, R.H. (1983). "Male Police Resistance to Female Police." In M. Doskow and G. Cordner (eds.) *Visions of Disorder.* Baltimore: University of Baltimore Honors Monograph Series.

Charles, M. (1981). "The Performance and Socialization of Female Recruits in the Michigan State Police Training Academy." *Journal of Police Science and Administration,* 9,2:209-223.

_____ (1982). "Women in Policing: The Physical Aspect." *Journal of Police Science and Administration,* 10,2:194-205.

_____ & K. Parsons (1978). "Female Performance in the Law Enforcement Function: A Review of Past Research, Current Issues and Future Potential." *Law and Order,* 26,1:18-22, 24, 27-28, 30, 32, 34, 36, 38, 40, 42-44, 46, 48, 50, 54-56.

Davis, J.A. (1984). "Perspectives on Policewomen in Texas and Oklahoma." *Journal of Police Science and Administration,* 12,4:395-403.

Dorsey, R. & D. Giacopassi (1986). "Assessing Gender Differences in the Levels of Cynicism among Police Officers." *American Journal of Police,* 5,1:91-112.

Feinman, C. (1980). *Women in the Criminal Justice System.* New York: Praeger.

Fry, L. (1983). "A Preliminary Examination of the Factors Related to Turnover of Women in Law Enforcement." *Journal of Police Science and Administration,* 11,2:149-155.

_____ & S. Greenfield (1980) "Examination of Attitudinal Differences Between Policeman and Policewoman." *Journal of Applied Psychology,* 65,1:123-126.

Golden, K. (1981). "Women as Patrol Officers: A Study of Attitudes." *Police Studies,* 4:29-33.

Goldstein, H. (1977). *Policing a Free Society.* Cambridge, MA: Ballinger.

Grennan, S. (1987). "Findings on the Role of Officer Gender in Violent Encounters with Citizens." *Journal of Police Science and Administration,* 15,1:78-85.

Hamilton, M. (1925). "Woman's Place in the Police Department." *The American City,* 32:194-195.

Harris, M. (1926). "The Policewoman: A Discussion of the Proper Function of the Policewoman and Her Relationship to the Rest of the Department." *City Manager Magazine*:20-21.

Hickman, K.G. (1983). Measuring Job Performance Success for Female Officers of the Los Angeles Police Department. Unpublished doctoral dissertation, Claremont Graduate School, Los Angeles.

Homant, R. (1983). "The Impact of Policewomen on Community Attitudes Toward Police." *Journal of Police Science and Administration,* 11,1:16-22.

_____ & D. Kennedy (1985). "Police Perceptions of Spouse Abuse: A Comparison of Male and Female Officers." *Journal of Criminal Justice,* 13:29-49.

Horne, P. (1979). "Policewomen: 2000 A.D." *The Police Journal,* 52,1:344-357.

Hutzel, E. (1923). "The Work of a Policewoman." Proceedings of the Annual Congress of Correction of the American Prison Association, pp. 73-78.

Johns, C. (1979). "The Trouble with Women in Policing: Attitudes Aren't Changing." *Criminal Justice Review,* 4,1:33-40.

_____ & A. Barclay (1979). "Female Partners for Male Police: The Effect on Shooting Responses." *Criminal Justice and Behavior,* 6,4:327-338.

Jones, S. (1986). "Women Police: Caught in the Act." *Policing,* 2,2:129-140.

Kennedy, D. & R. Homant (1981). "Nontraditional Role Assumption and the Personality of the Policewoman." *Journal of Police Science and Administration,* 9,3:346-355.

_____ (1983). "Attitudes of Abused Women Toward Male and Female Police Officers." *Criminal Justice and Behavior,* 10:391-405.

Kerber, K., S. Andes & M. Mittler (1977). "Citizen Attitudes Regarding the Competence of Female Police Officers." *Journal of Police Science and Administration,* 5,3:337-347.

Kizziah, C. & M. Morris (1977). *Evaluation of Women in Policing Program: Newton, Massachusetts.* Oakland, CA: Approach Associates.

LaBeff, E. & L. Williams (1982). "Male Officer Reactions to Females in Patrol: The Case of a Small City." *American Journal of Police,* 2,1:73-89.

Linn, E. & B. Price (1985). "The Evolving Role of Women in American Policing." In A.S. Blumberg & E. Niederhoffer (eds.) *The Ambivalent Force: Perspectives on the Police,* pp. 69-80. New York: Holt, Rinehart and Winston.

Liss, J. & S. Schlossman (1984). "The Contours of Crime Prevention in August Vollmer's Berkeley." *Research in Law, Deviance and Social Control,* 6:79-107.

Lord, L. (1986). "A Comparison of Male and Female Peace Officers' Stereotypic Perceptions of Women and Women Peace Officers." *Journal of Police Science and Administration,* 14,2:83-97.

McGeorge, J. & J. Wolfe (1976). "A Comparison of Attitudes Between Men and Women Police Officers: A Preliminary Analysis." *Criminal Justice Review,* 1,2:21-33.

Martin, C. (1979). "Women Police: A Survey of Education, Attitudes, Problems." *Journal of Studies in Technical Careers,* 1,3:220-227.

Martin, S. (1980). *Breaking and Entering: Policewomen on Patrol.* Berkeley: University of California.

―――――― (1990). *On the Move: The Status of Women in Policing.* Washington, DC: Police Foundation.

Melchionne, T. (1974). "The Changing Role of Policewomen." *The Police Journal,* 47:340-358.

Milton, C. (1975). "Women in Policing." In J.T. Curran & R.H. Ward (eds.) *Police and Law Enforcement: 1973-1974,* vol. 2, pp. 230-245. New York: AMS Press.

―――――― (1978). "The Future of Women in Policing." In A.W. Cohn (ed.) *The Future of Policing,* pp. 185-204. Beverly Hills, CA: Sage Publications.

―――――― , A. Abramowitz, L. Crites, M. Gates, E. Mintz, & G. Sandler (1974). *Women in Policing: A Manual.* Washington, DC: Police Foundation.

Mishkin, B. (1981). "Female Police in the United States." *The Police Journal,* 54:22-33.

Morash, M. (1986). "Perspective: Understanding the Contributions of Women to Police Work." In L.A. Radelet, *The Police and the Community,* 4th edition, pp. 290-294. New York: Macmillan.

―――――― & J. Greene (1986). "Evaluating Women on Patrol: A Critique of Contemporary Wisdom." *Evaluation Review,* 10,2:230-255.

Odem, M. & S. Schlossman (1991). "Guardians of Virtue: The Juvenile Court and Female Delinquency in Early Twentieth-Century Los Angeles." *Crime & Delinquency,* 37:186-203.

Owings, C. (1925). "Women Police." *Public Health Nursing,* 17:246-247.

Pennsylvania State Police Department Headquarters (1973). *Pennsylvania State Police Female Trooper Study.* Harrisburg, PA: author.

Pigeon, H. (1929). "Woman's Era in the Police Department." *The Annals of the American Academy of Political and Social Science,* 232:249-254.

Pogrebin, M. (1986). "The Changing Role of Women: Female Police Officers' Occupational Problems." *The Police Journal,* 59,2:127-133.

Price, B. (1985). "Sexual Integration in American Law Enforcement." In W.C. Heffernan & T. Stroup (eds.) *Police Ethics: Hard Choices in Law Enforcement,* pp. 205-214. New York: John Jay Press.

———— & S. Gavin (1982). "A Century of Women in Policing." In B.R. Price & N.J. Sokoloff (eds.) *The Criminal Justice System and Women,* pp. 399-412. New York: Clark Boardman.

Remmington, P. (1983). "Women in the Police: Integration or Separation?" *Qualitative Sociology,* 6,2:118-135.

Rutland, C. (1978). Comparative Analysis of the Relationship Between Social Background Factors and Training Performance of Male and Female Security Specialists. Unpublished master's thesis, California State University, Sacramento.

Sherman, L. (1975). "An Evaluation of Policewomen on Patrol in a Suburban Police Department." *Journal of Police Science and Administration,* 3,4:434-438.

Sichel, J., L. Friedman, J. Quint, & M. Smith (1978). *Women on Patrol: A Pilot Study of Police Performance in New York City.* Washington, DC: National Institute of Law Enforcement and Criminal Justice.

Snortum, J. & J. Beyers (1983). "Patrol Activities of Male and Female Officers as a Function of Work Experience." *Police Studies,* 6,1:36-42.

Steffensmeier, D. (1979). "Sex Role Orientation and Attitudes Toward Female Police." *Police Studies,* 2,1:39-42.

Sterling, B. & J. Owen (1982). "Perception of Demanding Versus Reasoning: Male and Female Police Officers." *Personality and Social Psychology Bulletin,* 8,2 (June):336-340.

Taylor, A. (1974). "Women Police." *The New York Times* (November 2):34. In C. Potholm & R. Morgan (eds.) (1976) *Focus on Police: Police in American Society,* pp. 207-212. New York: John Wiley and Sons.

United States Department of Justice (1984-1989). *Uniform Crime Reports for the United States* (annual volumes). Washington, DC: author.

Van Wormer, K. (1981). "Are Males Suited to Police Patrol Work?" *Police Studies,* 3,4:41-44.

Vega, M. & I. Silverman (1982). "Female Police Officers as Viewed by their Male Counterparts." *Police Studies,* 5:31-39.

Vollmer, A. (1930). "Meet the Lady Cop." *The Survey,* 63:702-703.

Walker, S. (1977). *A Critical History of Police Reform: The Emergence of Professionalism.* Lexington, MA: D.C. Heath.

Warner, R., B. Steel & N. Lovrich (1989). "Conditions Associated with the Advent of Representative Bureaucracy: The Case of Women in Policing." *Social Science Quarterly,* 70,3:562-578.

Weisheit, R. (1987). "Women in the State Police: Concerns of Male and Female Officers." *Journal of Police Science and Administration,* 15,2:137-144.

Weldy, W. (1976). "Women in Policing: A Positive Step Toward Increased Police Enthusiasm." *The Police Chief,* 43:46-47.

Wexler, J. & D. Logan (1983). "Sources of Stress Among Women Police Officers." *Journal of Police Science and Administration,* 11,1:46-53.

Wexler, J. & V. Quinn (1985). "Considerations in the Training and Development of Women Sergeants." *Journal of Police Science and Administration,* 13,2:98-105.

9

Training

Keith N. Haley
Ohio Peace Officer Training Council

INTRODUCTION

Training and learning are lifelong pursuits in law enforcement. A police officer attempting to do his job properly needs to be proficient in dozens of academic and skill areas. Even the seemingly simple process of using the straight baton to assist in making an arrest can frustrate the unskilled officer. And "Handcuff 101," the frequent object of ridicule by many academics, is a real course; it requires diligence to learn how to apply handcuffs safely and effectively in a variety of settings and circumstances.

As other professionals, police officers need to stay current with the latest research and best-recommended professional practices. To do anything less puts the officer, his employer, and the community at great risk. Training is the great equalizer upon which the burden rests to prepare and maintain a capable law enforcement officer. But training cannot overcome everything. Communities must select recruits who have both the potential for learning the requisites of police work and the motivation to serve citizens and visitors in their localities.

What are we trying to accomplish in law enforcement training? The answer to this question, as with so many others in policing, finds its origin in how one perceives the role of the American peace officer. Police officers are community leaders with broad discretion. Wilson (1968) describes the critical nature of law enforcement decisions, often involving life and death, honor and dishonor, blame and exoneration. The decision to arrest or not in a domestic dispute involves all of these values. Another major feature of the police officer's role is its problem-solving nature. Police officers are socio-logical and technological problem solvers. Show up at the scene of a multi-ple-car, fatal accident in a congested area and you will see good officers resolving many problems.

There are, of course, many other versions and features of the police role. Police are powerful people. They need to be great listeners and com-municators, even to the extent of being what one writer described as street-corner politicians (Muir, 1977). Their work often is done in virtual isolation, out of the view of their supervisors and the public. Much of what police do is "dirty work" (Van Maanen, 1973), work that many of us do not want to do ourselves or even see performed. Finally, we need to remem-ber that law enforcement work is dangerous and requires courageous people who will accept such risks.

The conventional perspective on training is to divide it into basic and advanced categories. Basic or recruit training is expected to prepare new officers for the initial demands of police work by providing at least mini-mum levels of knowledge and skills. No one expects a recruit to compete with a veteran patrol officer who has learned much of his craft ("what works") by responding to thousands of radio calls over a career. Typically, recruit training involves several hundred hours of training and often includes some field training in which recruits ride with veteran officers who act as coaches and usually submit some kind of evaluation of their pupils. Recruit training in Ohio, Michigan, California, and many other states con-sists of more than one hundred individual topics.

Advanced training in many agencies and states is a potpourri. What do you need to learn to be proficient in police patrol work, investigation, and all of the other specialties demanded of a modern, progressive law enforce-ment agency? Naturally, weapons and self-defense tactics are important and officers need to remain adept at performing these maneuvers. But advanced training also might include topics such as occult crime investigations, street gangs, domestic violence, legal updates, computer-related crimes, conflict management, child pornography, pursuit driving, electronic surveillance, and so forth. At the Ohio Peace Officer Training Academy in London, Ohio, advanced training includes nearly 400 course sections and 200 titles a year on almost every subject conceivably related to the diverse patrol, investiga-tive, and administrative responsibilities of law enforcement agencies.

Training or Education for Police Officers?

The argument still lingers over whether police officers should be trained or educated. What sense there is in perpetuating this argument is not clear. Police officers need both, and where the training and education occur is irrelevant. Some colleges and universities have resisted offering "training" for law enforcement officers on their campuses and, if it is conducted, it is often not granted academic credit. Somewhat ironically, these same colleges and universities give credit for work-oriented programs in dental services, hospitality management, accounting, engineering, surveying, and secretarial services.

Fortunately, the strength of this opposition at the university level may be waning as criminal justice and law enforcement mature as academic disciplines. If you conceive the police role as one having broad discretion and accept the fact that police are community leaders, there can be little question that officers need a solid educational foundation from which to make their decisions about community life. Higher education provides that foundation. Police officers are problem solvers in a diverse number of circumstances, however. In some situations there is a specific objective that needs to be achieved, and specific methods that should, or should not, be used. Consequently, training that provides the specialized instruction required to achieve clear-cut ends is also needed. All professions have such objectives.

There is a tremendous variety of training programs and opportunities available to recruit and experienced officers throughout America. There have been, however, few rigorous studies on the effectiveness of this training, student course evaluations notwithstanding. When the mandate and workload of most police agencies in America are considered, it is reasonable to expect that the academic and consultant communities will be tapped more and more in the future to conduct comprehensive evaluations of police training programs.

TRADITIONAL AND PRESENT PRACTICES IN TRAINING

Everyone knows how police work used to be learned. Police recruits, often chosen for their physical prowess or political connections, were sworn in, issued their guns and badges, and sent out into the community, often alone. The survivors learned under their own direction. When recruits were fortunate enough to be assigned to an experienced partner, the worry became: What experiences were passed on to the new, impressionable officer? At a national conference in Cincinnati the former chief of police of two large southern cities described for the audience his first night on the job in one of those cities during the 1950s. He went to roll call, met his partner, and headed for the patrol car. They proceeded immediately to a house of prostitution where the senior officer opened the glove box of the car, took out a bottle of whiskey, and then told the new officer to listen to the radio and to come in and get him if they were called. The first class was over and a "lesson" was learned.

Not all on-the-job training experiences went so poorly. But throughout the 1950s and 1960s many successful police officers learned their profession under the tutelage of a more experienced officer with little or no formal academy training. Though there were agencies at that time that had three- to six-month academy programs, by no means was that the norm for preparation for police work.

Today a minimum number of hours, nearly 400 on the average, is required to work as a peace officer in any of the states. A few states still permit the officer to take up to 6 months or a year to complete recruit training while working on the job, provided the officer undergoes some initial instruction in critical areas such as laws of arrest, search and seizure, firearms, and first aid. The liability concerns alone make such a procedure very risky and will undoubtedly account for its demise in the near future. There are, of course, many police academy programs, usually in large municipal and state agencies, which are six months or longer and have been such for years.

The length and content of recruit training are influenced by many factors beyond merely what is needed to go to work. Police recruits are usually paid nearly full salaries; the time they spend in the academy is time they are not on the street doing police work. Police executives want good training but it needs to be only long enough to give the new officers what they "need," a criterion not easily discerned. Then there is a scarcity of funding which creates pressure for a shorter training period. Smaller communities more often than not have training programs which are shorter than those in larger metropolitan areas with sizable tax bases. The type of community, history of the department, and expectations of the citizenry also have an impact on the length and quality of the training program. Still, there are far too many citizens who simply want to see more cops on the street and care little about the kind of training those officers receive.

The Minimum and Consensus Issue

With the advent of peace officer standards and training commissions (POSTs) in the late 1950s, state legislatures began to mandate minimum hours and content of recruit training. This initiated a neverending argument. The minimum amount of knowledge or skill needed in one community of the state may far exceed the need in another community under the jurisdiction of the POST agency. If a city, for example, has trained emergency medical technicians within minutes of any address in its jurisdiction, it is reasonable to assume that a large amount of first aid training would not be necessary for police recruits. If, however, deputy sheriffs or state troopers are miles from such capable assistance, then they would require considerably more first aid training. The same problem could be posed concerning crime scene processing. Communities with specialized personnel to do this work would likely resist lengthy units on this subject in recruit training. Regardless of what results from job analyses of different law enforcement officers' work, a consensus has to be reached on a state-mandated minimum in all of the subject areas and on a total number of hours, if a statewide curriculum is to be established. Political influences are factors in making those decisions.

Determining the amount of hours in each required subject, of course, affects what is taught. The very next hour of training that would have been taught above a state-mandated minimum may have been the hour that taught a skill or practice that could have saved an officer's or a citizen's life. Such decisions made about training are not trivial, to say the least.

Peace Officer Standards and Training Commissions

With the creation of the California Peace Officer Standards and Training Commission in 1959 (Christian & Edwards, 1985), a movement was launched to expand the role of state governments in determining personnel qualifications and training requirements for police officers. Peace Officer Standards and Training (POST) agencies grew from small organizations in the 1960s to agencies with several divisions, employing dozens of people, and expending millions of dollars each year on training and the development of personnel standards.

When POST commissions and agencies are examined, a number of structural features and differences in authority can be noted. First, not all POST commissions have the authority to set training and personnel standards. In the states with strong local political control, such as Ohio and Pennsylvania, the POSTs set only training minimums and requirements. Secondly, some POSTs oversee a broader jurisdiction than law enforcement, as evidenced by the inclusion in their titles and missions of the areas of criminal justice, corrections, and public safety. With the heightened interest in local corrections, peace officer standards and training commissions will continue to become more involved in this area. Finally, a number of states have included the terms "local" or "municipal" in the official titles of their POSTs, indicating that their standards and training requirements may not apply to state-level law enforcement agencies.

Creating and Maintaining a Basic Training Curriculum

Progressive municipal and county police agencies as well as POST commissions spend a great deal of time and money to determine what the basic training curriculum should be and to keep it current. While many fine training programs have been developed by experts in a field who know exactly what needs to be taught, conventional wisdom has relied on the job task analysis and subsequent processes to arrive at a valid and reliable training system. The system normally consists of a number of steps:

(1) a task analysis of work performed by a representative sample of officers;

(2) the identification and grouping of knowledge, skills, and abilities necessary to perform the tasks;

(3) the development of student educational objectives; and

(4) the construction of a curriculum that teaches the educational objectives and of tests that measure achievement.

TRENDS AND REFORMS

The Blurring of Education and Training

Perhaps there has been no greater influence on law enforcement training in the past several decades than higher education. The federal Law Enforcement Education Program (LEEP) of the 1960s and 1970s was partially responsible. Officers with baccalaureate and graduate degrees are no longer anomalies among police training staff and executive ranks, even if not yet the norm within many patrol and investigative divisions.

What has occurred in effect is a blurring between law enforcement training and education. A realization has occurred that effective police officers need to understand the major findings of the social sciences, the political process in a democracy, and the law. Booking a prisoner and taking fingerprints are clearly training needs, but understanding the nature of a community undergoing conflict and change requires broader theoretical underpinnings. Police officers can now get that knowledge in training academies and through education in mature criminal justice and law enforcement degree programs.

An ongoing cross-fertilization is taking place between law enforcement training and higher education. Former and current police trainers often are found on the rosters of criminal justice faculty, and once-distant criminal justice faculty with all of the respectable credentials are often seen teaching in basic and advanced classes at academies. In addition, there has been an increased academic interest in training; one example is the steadily growing curiosity of criminal justice faculty in the study of law enforcement training programs. A number of papers were given on the subject at recent annual meetings of the Academy of Criminal Justice Sciences. If this trend continues, law enforcement training programs are bound to benefit from the attention.

Student Performance Objectives

The whole world seems to have become objectified. Once the sole province of the military, now businesses, universities, teachers, counselors, and even police trainers attempt to spell out, in clearly defined terms, what they are trying to accomplish. Few people have not encountered behavioral objectives. In law enforcement training the student performance objectives (SPO) movement has had the desirable result. We can now place in the hands of students and instructors exactly what needs to be accomplished. In a field that is replete with "war stories" something was needed to keep many instructors and students on track.

Essentially, the behavioral objective format calls upon instructors to state:

(1) what the student will be able to do or know when instruction is completed;

(2) under what conditions students should be able to demonstrate their learning; and

(3) the criteria for judging successful performance.

Generally, academics and others who have examined police training materials developed in the SPO format have been impressed. It certainly beats "winging it," an occasional practice witnessed in the university classroom and other learning venues.

Training and Technology

Inevitably, all of the technology that has reached public and private education can be found in law enforcement training. The results have been good for the most part. With so many topics and specialties, police officers are not capable of keeping abreast of new developments on their own. Neither can training staff produce all of the classroom and simulation exercises necessary to be adequate to the task. Thus, the development of instructional resources outside specific training programs has become common.

Increasingly we are living in a video world. Television and the VCR have put at most people's fingertips the opportunity to see programs on every conceivable topic. In that regard, satellite television training has made a major contribution to law enforcement. One of the innovators has been the Law Enforcement Satellite Television Network (LESTN), a cooperative venture of the Kansas City Police Department and the Federal Bureau of Investigation. Training programs of two to three hours now can reach thousands of police officers at several hundred viewing sites across the nation. Even better, the programs can be taped and replayed for officers in future training programs.

As is the case with other aspects of police training, the private sector has become increasingly involved in new technological applications. LETN, the Law Enforcement Television Network, based in Carrollton, Texas, began broadcasting in July of 1989. The proprietor is Wescott Communications, a leader in business television. For a monthly fee from subscribers, LETN will broadcast law enforcement training as well as news and information 24 hours a day, five days a week. Six regularly scheduled shows appear daily on LETN along with occasional specials lasting an hour or more. LETN now has nearly 2,000 subscribing agencies throughout the nation, with the states of Texas, Ohio, and Florida having the most subscribers.

One study has shown that subscribers are pleased with LETN's programs and scheduling convenience (Haley, 1990). The network also has proved receptive to subscriber suggestions for programs and changes, no doubt a key to its expanding market.

Interactive video technology has allowed police students to sense the reality of a street situation without having to experience it firsthand or to reproduce a costly simulation. One popular training simulation is the Firearms Training System, or FATS, which allows officers the opportunity to engage in "shoot-don't shoot" situations that are street-based.

Programmed instruction on the computer is available on many subjects related to law enforcement. In both beginning and advanced training this allows the instruction to be repeated and the student to work at his or her own pace. Documentation of the training program is relatively simple to accomplish by merely producing the instructional program.

Cooperation for Training Effectiveness

No person or agency has all of the answers as to what is needed or what works in training. Cooperation among law enforcement and other public service agencies is common. There are myriad examples of this shared effort and service to the police training process. Of course, the Federal Bureau of Investigation has one of the longest records of aiding local and state police agencies (Deakin, 1988).

The Federal Law Enforcement Training Center (FLETC) in Glynco, Georgia is now the focal point for the bulk of the federal government's training effort. Under its parent agency, the Department of the Treasury, it provides hundreds of training courses for nearly all of the federal law enforcement agencies as well as staffing an Office of State and Local Training which provides local law enforcement agencies from across the nation the opportunity to acquire knowledge and skills not available in their region of the country. In 1985, 16,122 students were trained at FLETC (Federal Law Enforcement Training Center, 1985).

This same kind of cooperation among agencies relative to training is available in every state. Often the state police, the bureau of investigation, large municipal agencies, or a POST academy offer training resources and opportunities to other agencies and their personnel.

The Field Training Officer

Often an old idea can be improved upon—police agencies are once again relying on experienced patrol officers to help train new recruits (McCampbell, 1986). Traditionally, the question was, "Will the new officer learn good habits or bad habits from the veteran?" Over the years, refinements in this learning process have occurred to the point that field training is a standard practice in many agencies. But instead of leaving the specifics of that training up to whichever officer happens to have the most seniority, field training officers (FTOs) are now carefully selected and trained. Also, objectives and lessons are now clearly developed which expose recruits to a range of duties and experiences which help them prepare for the day when they will graduate from the academy and no longer be under the scrutiny of a probationary period. This comprehensive approach to field training has increased in popularity and effectiveness and has resulted in FTOs becoming true members of the academy staff.

ISSUES AND CONSTRAINTS IN TRAINING

While the opportunities for training in law enforcement have been prolific, preparing and maintaining police officers in a state of readiness for the demands of their work is not without some lingering issues and constraints.

The Burden of Liability

The risk of being sued in law enforcement has increased dramatically. In 1967, it was one chance in 200. By 1976, it had increased to one in 40; by 1987, it was estimated to be one in 20 (Foster, 1988). In 1983, there were 25,000 misconduct actions filed against the police in state and federal courts (Schmidt, 1985).

Whether to provide training is no longer the issue; police officers in all capacities must be adequately prepared to perform their duties (Barrineau, 1987). While most police leaders and commentators have not thought of it as a blessing in disguise, perhaps the ubiquitous Section 1983 civil liability lawsuit may generate as much progress in law enforcement and its training activities as all of the rhetoric and standard-setting clamor emanating from blue ribbon commissions and accreditation agencies. The "big wallop" of the lawsuit may be just the right weapon to get the attention of those who are recalcitrant or timid about improving standards and training for police personnel.

The Paramilitary Model for Policing and Training

Most police officers in America work in uniform in an organization whose structure and policies are paramilitary in nature. Again, the role of the police officer comes into question. For all of the innovation and experimentation with community-oriented policing models, which most often de-emphasize the military features of operation, police agency personnel remain uniformed, operating under policies, procedures, and practices that resemble those of military organizations. With the need for patrol officers to respond rapidly and effectively to order maintenance and criminal situations, the paramilitary resemblance is not likely to go away. Moreover, police agencies have such diverse responsibilities that policies and rules are necessary and they need to be followed. That requires discipline of at least one variety and paramilitary training and direction have a record of instilling this quality.

What effect a more civilianized approach to training and operations would have on the success of police agencies is not clear. There seem to be as many ways to manage a police agency as there are ways to run a business or school. All methods have experienced some success and the energy expended in the argument over military versus non-military policing models seems to be wasted.

THE NEED FOR RESEARCH IN POLICE TRAINING

Virtually all of the research conducted on training and available in the police literature has been descriptive in nature and does not tell us what really works. From several sources we know that at one time much of the recruit and advanced training consisted of technical and skill training with little emphasis in the human relations aspect of policing (President's Commission on Law Enforcement and the Administration of Justice, 1967; Saunders, 1970; Harris, 1973). Carte and Carte (1976) provide an excellent account of the influence on training of police reformer August Vollmer. We also know that national commissions and POSTs have been successful in increasing the number of hours of training for recruits and in implementing advanced training of various kinds in many states and in individual agencies. Several types of validation studies have been done in states to attempt to determine if mandated recruit curricula adequately prepare students to perform the tasks demanded in police work. One such study (Jurkanin, 1989) found that the Illinois recruit training curriculum was successful in preparing recruits, although some lessons were found in need of revision.

Much of the research on training has been done in conjunction with discussions of the police role and the socialization process for new officers. Logically that is the place to start. But given that the police role does vary, if ever so slightly, among agencies across the nation, it may be futile to keep wrangling about the one best role description and better to focus on what the police function is in specific agencies. There has been a tendency to overgeneralize when trying to identify the basic nature of police work (Muir, 1977). What is needed are more studies about what, in fact, works to prepare officers for the dozens of tasks they are going to perform regularly throughout their careers. How best should we be preparing recruits to intervene in domestic disputes, juvenile problems, traffic accidents, situations requiring emergency medical treatment, crimes in progress, and so on? The academic community would be of great service in assisting law enforcement and their communities if they could provide this assistance in the form of evaluation research.

If training does have the effect on recruits and older officers that most commentators think that it does, what do we know about the learning styles of officers at various stages in their careers and the teaching methods which work best in relation to those styles? Muir (1977) found in his study of the Laconia Police Department, that, once exposed to a more open and discussion-oriented approach to training, veteran officers saw value in in-service training and would willingly express their opinions and participate in other positive ways.

Perhaps even more important is the initiation of research on who makes the capable trainer in police organizations (Berg, 1990). What do we know about the characteristics of the successful police trainer? What are the best ways to prepare the trainer? It certainly takes more than looking good in the uniform and being able to tell a few entertaining stories.

There are unlimited research opportunities concerning training for faculty who are willing to work with police agencies and POST commissions. We will know a lot more about what works in training when the academic community and practitioners establish closer relationships.

SUMMARY AND CONCLUSIONS

The pursuit of knowledge and the acquisition of skills are lifelong endeavors for professional police officers. Successful performance as a police officer in American society, albeit slightly different in various communities, demands no less. It has become as common for an officer to attend in-service training at his agency or on a university campus as it once was for him to accept a free meal.

Police officers at all stages of their careers need to be trained and educated. There are specific objectives to be achieved on virtually every radio call, and training can be designed to help achieve those objectives. Yet there are also occasions where police agents need solid social, legal, and philosophical foundations to render good decisions in the complex situations they encounter.

Law enforcement training has undergone substantial improvement in the last several decades. More time and money have been spent on the effort and there has been increased cooperation among law enforcement agencies to produce excellent training programs. POST commissions and agencies have helped bring about more cooperation and have eased the financial burden to localities for training in many states. Finally, the development of clearly defined student performance objectives, lesson plans and other instructional resources, and improved examination procedures for academy training have brought the recruit and in-service learning process out of the realm of storytelling and into the area of sound educational practice.

But all of this is not to say that problems and issues do not remain. Police agencies must continue to hold the line on valid employment qualifications and attract motivated personnel. Secondly, increasing civil liability concerns over training have had their effects. The results have been positive in the sense that training is now often conducted more carefully, but for agencies that have been tagged with the bills for financial awards in these cases, the burdens have been substantial. Finally, the nation continues to argue over the relative merits of various policing styles, the military nature of most police agencies being one of the major issues. Perhaps our energy could be better spent. So much time has already been devoted to these studies with little meaningful change resulting.

Not much rigorous research has been conducted by academics or practitioners on the effectiveness of recruit and in-service training. What has been done has been largely institutional and not available in widely circulating journals and papers. We also need to know the desirable qualifications to be a law enforcement trainer. Finally, the law enforcement and academic communities need to establish closer relations in order that they don't find themselves working at cross-purposes. Emphasis on the superordinate goal of preparing capable police officers for their profession should draw the two communities together.

REFERENCES

Barrineau, H. (1987). *Civil Liability in Criminal Justice. Cincinnati:* Pilgrimage.

Berg, B. (1990). "Who Teaches Police? A Typology of Police Instructor Styles." *American Journal of Police,* 9,3.

Carte, G. & E. Carte (1975). *Police Reform in the United States.* Berkeley, CA: University of California Press.

Christian, K. & S. Edwards (1985). "Law Enforcement Standards and Training Councils." *Journal of Police Science and Administration,* 13(1):1-9.

Deakin, J. (1988). *Police Professionalism: The Renaissance of American Law Enforcement.* Springfield, IL: Charles C Thomas.

Federal Law Enforcement Training Center (1985). *1985 Annual Report.* Glynco, GA: author.

Foster, B. (1988). "Suing the Cops: Issues and Trends in Police Malpractice Litigation." Paper presented to the Academy of Criminal Justice Sciences, San Francisco, CA, March.

Harris, R. (1973). *The Police Academy: An Inside View.* New York: John Wiley and Sons.

Haley, K. (1990). "Real Cop Shows on TV: Early Reactions to LETN, The Law Enforcement Television Network." Paper presented to the Academy of Criminal Justice Sciences, Denver, March.

Jurkanin, T. (1989). "Does the Illinois Minimum Standards Basic Law Enforcement Training Curriculum Prepare Recruits for Police Work: A Survey Study." Paper presented to the Academy of Criminal Justice Sciences, Washington, DC, March.

McCampbell, M.S. (1986). "Field Training for Police Officers: State of the Art." *Research in Brief.* Washington, DC: National Institute of Justice.

Muir, W.K. (1977). *Police: Street Corner Politicians.* Chicago: University of Chicago Press.

National Advisory Commission on Criminal Justice Standards and Goals (1973). *Task Force on Police.* Washington, DC: U.S. Government Printing Office.

Saunders, C. (1970). *Upgrading the American Police.* Washington, DC: Brookings Institution.

Schmidt, W. (1985). "Section 1983 and the Changing Face of Police Management." In W.A. Geller (ed.) *Police Leadership in America.* New York: Praeger.

Van Maanen, J. (1973). "Observations on the Making of a Policeman." *Human Organization.* 32:407-418.

Wilson, J.Q. (1968). *Varieties of Police Behavior.* Cambridge, MA: Harvard University Press.

10

Leadership and Management

Mittie D. Southerland
Eastern Kentucky University

Elizabeth Reuss-Ianni
Institute for Social Analysis

INTRODUCTION

Early American police worked with little direction or supervision other than their rule books. As a result, they acted rather independently of management but with regard for the political nature of their jobs. There was no job security because police were hired, dismissed, and replaced by those in political power (often a police captain was responsible for selecting personnel for his section). Police personnel changed as frequently as politicians went in and out of office; therefore, positions of both supervisory and line personnel were tenuous (Uchida, 1989).

The professional movement markedly changed the face of police leadership and management. O.W. Wilson successfully advocated professional policing through the use of Weber's principles of bureaucratic management. Wilson authored the classic book *Police Administration,* first published in 1950, which became the standard for police leadership and management for the next two decades. The professional police agency, which functioned using authoritarian and impersonal management and bureaucratic principles, became known as the *traditional* police organization. Advocates of change began to challenge this model in the mid-1960s, calling for more participatory styles of management. Since we have little or no research data indicating to what degree, if any, police organizations have moved away from the traditional mode of leadership, it can be argued that the challenge for change continues. Troubling is the fact that we still know little about the current status and effectiveness of police leadership and management.

LEADERSHIP STYLE AND ORGANIZATIONAL VALUES

Leadership style and organizational values and policy are used to shape and control police behavior. Employee satisfaction and organizational goal accomplishment may depend on the style of leadership and the extent to which the values, objectives, policies, and programs of management agree with the values and objectives of the officer on the street.

Leadership Style

A variety of leadership models exist in the general management literature. Best known among these are Likert's Leadership Systems (1961, 1967), Blake and Mouton's Managerial Grid (1964), House and Mitchell's Path-Goal Theory (1974), Hersey and Blanchard's Situational Leadership (1969, 1988), and Blanchard, Zigarmi, and Zigarmi's Situational Leadership II (1985). Figure 10.1 compares these styles, except for Path-Goal Theory which does not include specific styles.

Likert's Leadership Systems

Likert examined management in a number of industrial plants to discover the styles of leadership used by various managers and the relative effectiveness of these styles. He identified four types of leadership on a continuum from low leader-employee interaction and employee involvement to high leader-employee interaction and employee involvement. Any leader could be categorized into one of four types. The styles from low involvement to high involvement are exploitive-authoritarian, benevolent-authoritarian, consultative, and participative. Likert's evaluation of employee performance and management style revealed that the consultative and participative styles were much more effective than either of the authoritarian styles. The participative style was the most effective of all the styles. Effective management was defined as the type of management which results in high productivity from the perspective of other managers.

Figure 10.1
Comparison of Leadership Styles

Likert's Single-Dimension Style

| Exploitive-
Authoritarian | Benevolent-
Authoritarian | Consultative | Participative |

Two-Dimension Styles

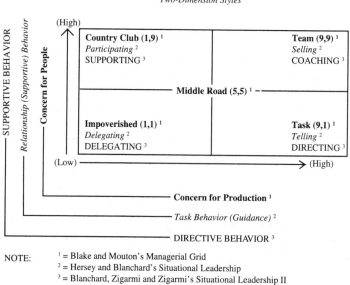

NOTE: [1] = Blake and Mouton's Managerial Grid
  [2] = Hersey and Blanchard's Situational Leadership
  [3] = Blanchard, Zigarmi and Zigarmi's Situational Leadership II

Blake and Mouton's Managerial Grid

Blake and Mouton's two-dimensional Managerial Grid presents five different types of leader behavior based on the leader's concern for task production (horizontal axis) and concern for relationship with employees (vertical axis). Four of the five styles are located in four separate quadrants and one style is in the center of the grid. From the most effective style to the least effective style the five types are: the Team leader (9,9), the Middle Road leader (5,5), the Task leader (9,1), the Country Club leader (1,9), and the Impoverished leader (1,1).

House and Mitchell's Path-Goal Theory

Path-Goal Theory is concerned with how the leader influences a subordinate's perception of work goals, personal goals, and paths to goal attainment. The leader's behavior is motivating or satisfying to the degree to which the leader's behavior increases the employee's goal attainment and clarifies the paths to goal achievement. The contingency here is task structure. With an unstructured task, employee satisfaction is highest when the leadership style is high on task behavior and low on relationship behavior; with a structured task, employee satisfaction is highest when the leadership style is low on task behavior and high on relationship behavior.

Hersey and Blanchard's Situational Leadership

Hersey and Blanchard see leadership style as situational, i.e., there is no single ideal leader behavior as advocated by Likert and by Blake and Mouton. For Hersey and Blanchard, certain leadership styles are appropriate or inappropriate given certain situations. Their model examines four dimensions, each of which is viewed as a separate continuum: the readiness level of the employee, the leader's task (guidance) behavior, the leader's relationship (supportive) behavior, and the effectiveness of the leader's behavior as measured by employee behavior. The readiness level of the employee determines the combination of task and relationship behavior which is appropriate. If the appropriate leader behavior is selected, the employee's behavior will be more effective than if a less appropriate leader behavior is used. Hersey and Blanchard's leader behaviors from high task (guidance) to low task behavior are Telling, Selling, Participating and Delegating. The Telling and Delegating behaviors are low on supportive behavior while the Selling and Participating behaviors are high on supportive behavior.

Blanchard, Zigarmi, and Zigarmi's Situational Leadership II

Situational Leadership II (SL2) differs primarily in terminology from Hersey and Blanchard's Situational Leadership. SL2 uses the terms Directing, Coaching, Supporting, and Delegating in place of Hersey and Blanchard's Telling, Selling, Participating, and Delegating. The SL2 terms tend to be more descriptive of the leader behavior categories. The dimensions of leader behavior in SL2 are called directive and supportive. The employee's development level is determined by examining the competence and commitment of the employee in terms of accomplishing organizational tasks. Directing is appropriate for low competence, high commitment employees; Coaching is appropriate for some competence, low commitment employees; Supporting is appropriate for high competence, variable commitment employees; and Delegating is appropriate for high competence, high commitment employees.

General Patterns

The styles most likely to be used in bureaucratic organizations are Likert's exploitive-authoritarian and benevolent-authoritarian styles, Blake and Mouton's task and impoverished styles, and the leader behaviors which are highly directive and low supportive regardless of the employee's development or needs in terms of the situational and contingency leadership models. The styles most likely to be used in participative organizations are Likert's consultative and participative styles, Blake and Mouton's team, middle road, and country club styles, and the leader behaviors which are highly supportive and low directive regardless of the employee's development or needs. They also are more likely to use the situational and contingency leadership models which appropriately combine directive and supportive behaviors according to the employee's development or needs.

Organizational Values and Culture

Rokeach (1973) defines values as enduring beliefs that certain, specific modes of conduct or states of existence are preferable. Organizational values refer to the beliefs, purpose, mission, and goals that define what is important in the organization. The value system organizes these concepts into a framework which allows individuals to know what is appropriate and acceptable behavior, i.e., what *means* are acceptable and what *ends* are to be sought. According to Ouchi (1981), organizational values include a set of beliefs about what kinds of solutions work well. The beliefs also identify who should make decisions and what kinds of activities the organization should or should not consider doing. These values and beliefs must be expressed in concrete ways if new members of the organization are to understand and believe them.

Thomas Watson, Jr., founder of IBM and an early proponent of organizational values, said:

> I firmly believe that any organization, in order to survive and achieve success, must have a sound set of beliefs on which it premises all its policies and actions. Next, I believe that the most important single factor in corporate success is faithful adherence to those beliefs. And, finally, I believe if an organization is to meet the challenge of a changing world, it must be prepared to change everything about itself except those beliefs as it moves through corporate life. In other words, the basic philosophy, spirit, and drive of an organization have far more to do with its relative achievements than do technological or economic resources, organizational structure, innovation, and timing. All these things weigh heavily in success. But they

> are, I think, transcended by how strongly the people in
> the organization believe in its basic precepts and how
> faithfully they carry them out (Peters & Waterman,
> 1982:280).

Peters and Waterman (1982) found that every excellent company they studied had a clear set of values and was serious about the process of shaping those values. They questioned whether it is possible to be excellent without "clarity on values and without having the right sorts of values" (1982:280). They identified the following seven values as the "right sorts of values" for organizations:

1. A belief in being the "best."
2. A belief in the importance of the details of execution, the nuts and bolts of doing the job well.
3. A belief in the importance of people as individuals.
4. A belief in superior quality and service.
5. A belief that most members of the organization should be innovators, and its corollary, the willingness to support failure.
6. A belief in the importance of informality to enhance communication.
7. Explicit belief in and recognition of the importance of economic growth and profits (1982:285).

In transmitting values to members of the organization, so that they are "bone-deep beliefs," the executive leader's role is critical. Peters and Austin (1985:212) give executives this advice:

> Be confident in your beliefs. Live them with integrity.
> Remember that the "small stuff" is all there is. It's a
> pretty tough message. If your convictions about people
> aren't all that clear and strong, then it's tough to be con-
> fident and consistent. Maybe that's the secret, for good or
> ill, after all.

Personnel selection is a logical starting point for assuring that employees can and will incorporate the organizational values into their belief systems. Peters (1987) stresses the importance of using the values of the organization to determine the criteria for personnel selection.

The culture of an organization is comprised of the symbols, ceremonies, and myths that communicate the organization's values and beliefs to its employees. "These rituals put flesh on what would otherwise be sparse and abstract ideas, bringing them to life in a way that has meaning and impact for a new employee" (Ouchi, 1981:35). When all personnel in the organization have the same set of values, a common culture results.

The common culture or shared philosophy results in everyone speaking a common language. Employees understand their rights and responsibilities as members of the organization, and they are aware of the degree to which they will participate in decision-making. These common understandings simplify the entire process of leadership and management.

The common culture develops as employees have a broad range of common (shared) experiences through which they can communicate subtly. Due to the common culture, each is able to correctly assume responses and agreements without having to negotiate them. This facilitates coordination and greatly simplifies decision-making and planning. Large numbers of people can be involved as active participants in decision-making and planning because they have an underlying agreement on philosophy, values, and beliefs. Shared responsibility is feasible only under the conditions of a common culture.

Ouchi (1981) found that the common culture was very important to the success of the companies he examined in the book *Theory Z*. Peters and Waterman (1984) also found the value system to be extremely important to successful companies. Without a strong value system, an organization's success is highly unlikely. The common value system depends on a strong executive to develop and transmit values to all employees, tightly controlling the values of the organization while exercising loose or no control on all other matters.

WHAT HAVE WE LEARNED?

There is no research to date that can definitively describe what works in police leadership and management. There are a few articles which indicate what forms of leadership might be more effective in terms of producing better police performance. Some of these are directed specifically at examining police leadership, others are more indirectly focused. We know something about the leadership styles used in policing, but we know more about what does not work than about what works in police management.

Leadership Style

Shanahan, Hunger, and Wheelen (1979) used Likert's Profile of Organizational Characteristics to assess style change in policing from 1974 to 1976 by obtaining responses of 171 members of police organizations who were attending the National Academy of the Federal Bureau of Investigation in January 1976. Subjects were asked to respond to each of the 51 items regarding the organization at the present time (1976) and two years earlier (1974). The results indicated that the officers placed their organizations close to the midpoint of the consultative style of leadership in 1976; they placed their organizations in the upper part of benevolent-authoritarian in 1974. The three categories which changed most were communication, training, and decision-making, suggesting a more participative style and openness to upward and lateral transfer of information.

Jermier and Berkes (1979) examined the role of police leaders from the perspective of Path-Goal theory in building employee morale through instrumental and supportive leadership in a police bureaucracy. They studied 158 police personnel, who represented a random cross-section of all police officers in a Midwestern police department with 800 sworn and civilian personnel. Leader participativeness and task variability were found to be highly significant predictors of subordinate job satisfaction and commitment to the organization. They also found that when tasks were perceived by subordinates as unpredictable, the subordinates preferred the leader to clarify their roles. Under these conditions, directive and participative role clarification improved job satisfaction; participative role clarification improved organizational commitment. When officers reported their tasks as predictable, role clarification was unnecessary and supportive leadership had the most positive outcome. Job satisfaction was enhanced with supportive leadership because of its role in conflict and stress reduction. Participation was most effective in increasing organizational commitment and job satisfaction when tasks were interdependent. However, when officers performed "one-person" tasks, formal leaders were more effective when they defined the officers' roles and provided performance feedback. This study highlighted the importance of participative and supportive leadership for building employee satisfaction and commitment to the organization.

Kuykendall and Unsinger (1982) used Hersey and Blanchard's Leader Effectiveness and Adaptability Description (LEAD) instrument to examine the leadership styles of 155 police managers from 104 different agencies at the beginning of seven managerial training programs in Arizona and California in 1978, 1979, and 1980. The managers were asked to respond to the described situations using available alternatives as they would actually respond to similar situations in their organizations. The managers "tended to be most effective in using styles with a high task emphasis (telling and selling) and least effective in the styles requiring a low task orientation (participating and delegating)" (1982:315). The delegating style was used least often—102 of the managers did not use the delegating style at all, while 31 used it in only one situation. Seventy-eight percent of the managers emphasized either the participating-selling or telling-selling combinations. The selling style was used more frequently than any other style, but managers tended to use more than one style.

Swanson and Territo (1982) administered the Managerial Grid questionnaire to 104 police supervisors and managers attending five workshops held in the southeastern United States between 1978 and 1980. The Team style was the most often preferred primary style (38% chose this style). The second most frequently chosen primary style was the Task style (28%). The most frequently selected backup style was Task (29%) with Middle Road a close second (25%). The most commonly occurring combination of primary and secondary styles was the Team as primary and Middle Road as secondary (17%).

Dunning and Hochstedler (1982) used 1973 survey data from the Dallas, Texas police department to examine the relationship between satisfaction and communication for 822 patrol officers. The officers in this department were generally satisfied with both the level and amount of horizontal and vertical communication offered by their immediate supervisors. They also were very satisfied with the work itself, their sense of achievement, the recognition they received, and their immediate supervisor. Dunning and Hochstedler were not particularly interested in the management style or officer's evaluation of management and did not discuss the findings relevant to those issues, yet for the present purpose this is the most interesting outcome of their research. The strongest correlations reported in the study were found in the association of two sets of variables. These were the associations

(1) between the officer's *satisfaction with the immediate supervisor* and the officer's satisfaction on seven indicators of *vertical communication with the immediate supervisor* and

(2) between the officer's satisfaction with *recognition given by the supervisor* and the officer's satisfaction with *vertical communication*.

Officers who evaluated their supervisor as a "bad manager" were more likely to evaluate vertical communication negatively while officers who evaluated their supervisor as "top notch" or "very competent" were more likely to evaluate vertical communication positively. The same pattern held for recognition.

Kuykendall (1985) reports the Managerial Grid responses of 255 police managers representing 165 law enforcement organizations. The survey instrument measured the grid response most and least characteristic of the manager on three situations in each of four managerial areas: philosophy of management, planning and goal-setting, implementation, and evaluation. The most prevalent style was Team followed by Task; 83 percent of the respondents' were classified in these areas. Backup styles were more evenly dispersed—Middle Road and Task styles constituted 57 percent of these responses. Kuykendall reported that the managers changed styles as they dealt with different managerial activities.

Roberg and Krichhoff (1985) used the Managerial Style Questionnaire (MSQ) and the Leader Behavior Description Questionnaire (LBDQ) as part of their evaluation of organizational conditions in two agencies. The instruments were administered to both sworn officers and management personnel. The MSQ measures the use of objectives by managers; the LBDQ measures consideration (relationship orientation) and initiating structure (task orientation). In the small police department the results indicated that "goals are not understood nor are they used to manage the organization. Supervisors neither show concern for organization members nor defined member's roles for them" (1985:142). The ratings for the sheriff's department were similar—the personnel rated leadership low in consideration and initiating structure (LBDQ) and low in goal use on the MSQ. Since this was not the primary interest of their study, Roberg and Krichhoff did not analyze the results further. The results as presented, though, seem to indicate that the leaders in these organizations functioned differently from the ways the managers in the other studies perceived their styles. These managers could be classified as Impoverished leaders in the Managerial Grid and certainly were not using the Directive styles of the situational models.

Auten's (1985) study of police management in the State of Illinois found that 63 percent of administrators believed that they used Likert's consultative style of management while 45 percent of command/supervisory personnel viewed the management styles of their administrators as benevolent-authoritarian. Operational personnels' assessments of management style fell between those of administrative and command/supervisory personnel—47 percent of operational personnel viewed management as consultative and 26 percent saw it as benevolent-authoritarian. Auten's work indicates that there are different perceptions of management style depending on the position one holds in the organization. Clearly those being managed view the style differently (more authoritarian) than those who are doing the managing.

Weisburd, McElroy, and Hardyman (1988) reported their observations of supervisory style in the New York City Police Department (NYPD) Community Patrol Officer Program pilot project. They described methods of supervision that were systematic, not bureaucratic. The leadership strategy was to evaluate the officer's knowledge of the community, involvement in the community, and ability to solve problems. The supervisor and officer jointly develop a work plan with objectives and strategies for lessening the priority problems they have identified. These plans serve as the context for encouraging the officer's initiative and judging results. The supervisory approach "also recognized the diversity of problems, desires and resources among neighborhoods patrolled, and permitted the supervision to take account of that diversity in judging the performance of police officers" (1988:45). The supervision described is very similar to the Situational Leadership concept and Contracting for Leadership Style (Hersey &

Blanchard, 1988; Blanchard et al., 1985). Weisburd et al. emphasize that supervisory style must differ as the assigned mission and tasks differ. The character of the CPO project was different from foot patrol and vastly dissimilar to traditional motorized patrol. Similarly, Wilson (1978) discovered differences in management style between the Federal Bureau of Investigation and the Drug Enforcement Administration, due primarily to differences in the nature of the tasks and missions of the two agencies.

Witte, Travis, and Langworthy (1990) surveyed the members of a number of small to medium-sized police departments in southern Ohio concerning their perceptions of the utility of participatory management for improving policing and the current level of practical support given participatory management by administrative personnel. They found that respondents at all ranks believed "in the theory of participatory management and its potential to improve the operations of current police departments" (1990:17), but they had not seen its reality in practice. Only those persons who were in positions of power to make decisions in the organizations and members of small police departments reported satisfaction with the level of participatory management in their departments.

Hoover and Mader (1990) surveyed Texas administrators about their views regarding the principles of excellence presented by Peters and Waterman (1982). They found that Texas administrators were very supportive of the principles of excellence advocated in the private sector management literature, yet these administrators feel impotent to implement the principles in their police agencies.

Southerland (1989) examined the leadership styles of police patrol sergeants in a Midwestern police department from the perspective of patrol personnel. A survey instrument was used to assess the degree to which police patrol sergeants in this department adhered to the principles of Situational Leadership II (SL2). Patrol personnel at all levels of the patrol division of the police department were asked to identify the assignment and control behavior of current patrol sergeants in their department. The survey presented eight supervisory situations (four assignment and four control). Patrol personnel were asked to respond from their perspective as to how the best patrol sergeant, worst patrol sergeant, and typical patrol sergeant in their organization would most likely respond to each of the situations. The survey results supported the usefulness of SL2 for police supervision. The best sergeants were perceived as using the most appropriate SL2 responses in both the control and assignment tasks, given the development level of the officers. The worst sergeants used the most unacceptable or least effective responses in both the control and assignment tasks according to SL2.

Southerland (1990) continued the examination of SL2 for use in the police patrol environment by examining officers' perceptions of first-line supervisory behavior in assignment and corrective situations in seven southern police agencies (N ranging from 13 to 159) with an overall N of 575 respondents. The results indicated no real differences across rank or across sites in the perceived best and worst supervisory responses. Responses indicated that officers, regardless of their levels of development, want and need direction to know the expectations of their supervisors. They also want and need support and encouragement. Further, they want to know when they have made mistakes and specifically what was done wrong and how to correct it. These results give general support to the SL2 model of supervision but indicate that officers want more direction and support than SL2 predicts. Further research is needed to detail the types and amounts of direction and support which should be provided in policing to accomplish organizational effectiveness and employee satisfaction.

If the perceptions of the respondents in the studies presented above are correct and are generally representative of police management styles in the United States, police management is much less autocratic than is generally believed. Yet, the studies also indicate a fairly strong bureaucratic orientation due to the relative avoidance of delegating and low-directing types of behavior. However, these studies are by no means conclusive and, because they are surveys, they give little understanding of operational leadership in the day-to-day police setting. The field studies of policing give a somewhat different view since they examine managerial style in context.

Organizational Values and Culture

All police personnel are responsible for implementing the policies and procedures of the organization. When the values and goals of the police agency are not shared by personnel at all levels of the organization (administrators, managers, supervisors, and officers), the police agency is in trouble; no one will really know what is supposed to be happening, much less what is actually happening. As a result, the goals cannot be achieved or, at best, they will be achieved inconsistently and unreliably. Research on bureaucratic organizations repeatedly suggests that the behavioral intentions of personnel in organizations often diverge from the formally stated organizational objectives. Wasserman and Moore (1988) reiterate this in their discussion of the relationship of values to contemporary policing. A major problem of police values to them is that the implicit values are often at odds with the explicit values of the police agency: "This breeds confusion, distrust, and cynicism rather than clarity, commitment, and high morale" (1988:1). A statement of values is only a starting point for them, yet they give us no direction for developing common cultures in policing.

The problematic nature of patrol officers learning the values and goals of the police organization is evident in Bayley and Bittner's research:

departmental policy is often not clearly expressed or understood. Supervisors indicate—sometimes subtly, sometimes directly—what they prefer by way of action. Officers are aware that what they normally do is not what "the sergeant" or "the lieutenant" would do. Officers cynically remark that calling a supervisor for assistance in a domestic fight usually produces "two domestics," one among civilians, another among police ... (1989:91).

Two Cultures of Policing

Based on over 18 months of observational research in two New York City Police precincts from 1976 to 1978, Reuss-Ianni (1983) concluded that, at least in that agency, the organization of policing is best described and understood in terms of the interaction of two distinct cultures: a street-cop culture and a management-cop culture. These two cultures are increasingly characterized by competing and often conflicting perspectives on policy, procedure, and practice in policing. In these competing cultures of policing, officers (street cops) adopt notions of their police responsibilities which conform with what the individual officers and their peers are willing to do but are not necessarily in concert with what police managers (management cops) want or expect them to do. The struggle between street-cop and management-cop values (goals and objectives) might be explained by two maxims prevalent in organization theory. First, workers are not really committed to decisions they feel they have no part in making. Second, subordinates attempt to free themselves as much as possible from organizational controls. The inevitable result is disaffection and disharmony in the workplace and conflict between managers and workers: between bosses and cops.

Traditionally, much of the research and literature on policing has described the workings of a monolithic single-cop culture that maintains and pervades all levels of the organization. The contrary notion of two cultures, however, has very different implications for command and control, for the introduction of new management and operational techniques, for new personnel policies and procedures, and for understanding the manner and method of the day-to-day "job" of policing. The existence of two cultures (street and management) in policing leads to conflict and competition in the organization. The management cops want one type of organization while the street cops want another. The strategies surrounding this "battle" may explain why change in some police organizations occurs more slowly than in others.

The street-cop culture of career cops is defined by a pervasive conception of a "good old days" of policing. In the good old days the public valued and respected the cop, fellow officers could be counted on, and the bosses at all levels were a part of a cohesive, interdependent police family. Cops were treated by the public and by their superior officers as professionals who knew their job and how best to get it done. Supervisors delegated the police function to officers and trusted them to accomplish their tasks. There was a code of shared understandings and conventions of behavior that bound everyone in the department from the top brass to the newest recruits. There was a common culture. The department also was integrated with and accommodated the political system which valued them and their culture. Because of its solidarity and integration into the political system, the department was (by and large) left to run its own affairs. This nostalgic sense of the good old days may or may not be an accurate or factual interpretation of the past, but the street cops Reuss-Ianni observed believe police work should still be organized and carried out that way today.

Street cops believe a number of forces have weakened the character and effectiveness of police work. According to these officers, contempt and suspicion rather than respect and confidence are experienced daily in the community and in the media. Frequent charges of brutality and corruption have led to distrust and suspicion among police officers. These and related concerns, rather than the mutuality of the old days, relates them to their bosses and the command structure.

From the perspective of street cops, management cops are police who have decided that the old way of running a police department is finished. They do not, like street cops, for example, regard community relations as "Mickey Mouse bullshit," but as something that must be done for politically expedient reasons if not for social ones. The management cop is sensitive to politics and public opinion and predictability in performance. It generally is believed by street cops that management cops and their political allies at city hall are tying the hands of the street cop, reducing their level of performance, and making it more difficult and dangerous to police the community.

The management-cop culture is bureaucratically juxtaposed to the street-cop culture; what was once a family is now a factory. The street cops say that the values and the real loyalties of their bosses are not to the men who they command, but to the social and political networks which embody management-cop culture. The upper echelons of administration control the setting of objectives without sufficiently considering either the demands of the environment or the recommendations from field officers, even when they have asked for officer input.

The street cops described management as being, in terms of the Managerial Grid, primarily concerned with production and not with relationships with officers. Street cops say that the new management cop is positively oriented toward public administration and looks to scientific management and its associated technologies for guidance on how to run the department. There is greater emphasis on accountability and productivity—on management processes and products that can be quantified and measured in a cost-effective equation.

There is a game-like quality in the present relationship between street-cop and management-cop cultures. The headquarters managers can mandate specific policies and procedures, but they cannot make street cops treat those policies and procedures seriously. The street cops who are still dedicated to the old ways of doing things are confused and often enraged at the apparent change in the rules of the game. They fight back with the traditional weapons of alienated employees—footdragging, sabotage, and stealing company time. If the managers have the authority but not the means for requiring serious acceptance of their programs and policies, neither do the workers have the power to outwit the managers altogether. The response is a further attempt to maneuver for position in the game. Dumping tickets, passing around arrests to whoever needs to "get on the sheet," breaking the picture tube on a stolen TV set when the guy they know—but cannot prove—to be "dirty" is carrying it down the street, are means of circumventing the formal rules of the game, as are the responses such as: "You want numbers, we'll give you numbers. You want to treat us like kids, try and catch us." And, "Why should we make you look good, what does it get us?" This response clearly denotes that, while most of them know they cannot possibly win the game, they still seek some small victory on the way down.

While there is some uneasy accommodation between these two cultures, they are increasingly in conflict, and this conflict isolates the precinct functionally, if not structurally, from headquarters. The isolation produces disaffection, strong stress reactions, increasing attrition of personnel, and growing problems of integrity. This in turn reinforces street-cop culture resistance to attempts by headquarters' managers to introduce organizational change. Most of the officers with whom Reuss-Ianni worked see the destruction of the street-cop culture as an inevitable outcome of the changing organizational character, and with obvious resignation say that this is what the bosses really want anyway because they can more easily control cops as individuals than as unified groups.

The existence of these two cultures of policing is of more than academic interest. Their incongruent value systems and the differences in their expectations are major factors in the growing alienation of the street cop. This displacement of quasi-familial relationships in which loyalties and commitments took precedence over the rule book by the more impersonal ideology of modern management is visible in other public service sectors as well. And wherever this shift occurs, it produces conflict which sooner or later must affect the way the public experiences services. These old and new cultures will most likely continue to coexist for some time.

Two Cultures of Management

The cultures of policing may be more complex than those described by Reuss-Ianni. Van Maanen (1989) discovered two very different supervisory-level cultures in operation in the organization he observed. He called these cultures the station house sergeant culture and the street sergeant culture. Station house sergeants are almost always at or near their work stations. Their role is to stand behind the officers assigned to them and take responsibility for the officer's conduct on the beat. They are concerned with motivating officers to fulfill their quotas, properly fill out their reports, stay in line with departmental rules and regulations, and answer calls within tolerable time limits. The supervisory style is relatively formal and distant.

Street sergeants stand alongside their officers. Their role is collegial and is enacted, not behind a desk or in an office, but on the streets. Street sergeants define their mission not in terms of their responsibility for the officers' behavior but for the territory they command. They view the objectives of their job in ways quite similar to the role of those whom they supervise.

According to Van Maanen (1989), both orientations are problematic from the perspective of the street cop. The street sergeant is often seen as a poacher who intrudes too frequently and competitively in the field where patrol officers feel they deserve autonomy. Station house sergeants are too preoccupied by the rule book and are unappreciative of situational differences that sometimes make the rules and regulations dangerous or irrelevant for guiding action in the field. Yet, both kinds of management cops have positive features. The street sergeant knows the score, knows what is happening on the beat, and is not "too persnickety about the legal niceties" surrounding policing. The station house sergeant can be located when a question arises or reports need to be adjusted or need signatures; they have more intradepartmental clout and are useful when an officer wants to change shifts, precincts, or partners; and they tend to have more favors than street sergeants for giving to officers they believe are deserving. Station house sergeants are easier to work for because they are more predictable than street sergeants.

Most police sergeants could be classified as station house sergeants. These station house sergeants view the street sergeant disdainfully as having a "patrolman's mentality." This patrolman's mentality seldom exists at the sergeant level and is even more rare further up the chain of command. Van Maanen (1989) believes that police officials should think of ways to preserve, not obliterate, the patrolman's mentality throughout the ranks.

> As it stands now, the care and close oversight of police work is a small, but regrettably undervalued part of what sergeants might do. Of course, most sergeants do see to it that at least some police work gets done and docu-

mented. But, as Bittner (1983) recently pointed out, few sergeants show much interest in whether or not such work is done well. This, perhaps more than anything else, is the central problem facing police command (Van Maanen, 1989:160).

The Scottish police sergeants observed by Currie (1988a, 1988b) exhibited many of the same characteristics as Van Maanen's street sergeants, while the managers and inspectors seemed more similar to Reuss-Ianni's management cops. These sergeants viewed their leadership role as fitting within the Team concept, i.e., they were to get the job done while looking out for the welfare of their constables (officers). Currie also found two distinctive types of sergeants—the county (rural) and the burgh (urban).

Transmission of Values

Values are transmitted in organizations through socialization. The socialization process occurs at all career stages, yet the effect of socialization during the breaking-in period is most significant for determining behavior due to the individual's vulnerability at this point—the officer has little operational knowledge, few guidelines to direct behavior, and too much or too little confidence. Numerous studies indicate that recruit socialization determines, to a great extent, the officer's later beliefs, attitudes, and behaviors (Van Maanen, 1978).

In the early 1970s, Van Maanen (1978) observed recruit socialization in a large bureaucratic metropolitan police department with over 1,500 uniformed officers and concluded that early police socialization is primarily a product of the training academy and the Field Training Officer (FTO). Van Maanen did not examine the role of supervisors in the process of organizational socialization and it has not yet been examined to any significant degree.

Van Maanen found that the paramilitary environment of group reward and punishment in the *training academy* promotes peer group solidarity. The "recruit soon learns it is his peer group rather than the 'brass' which will support him and which he, in turn, must support" (1978:299). The recruit also learns that formal rules and regulations are applied inconsistently, i.e., what is ignored in one case is punished in another case, and that when managers notice behavior, it will be to punish, not to reward.

Following the training academy, the probationary officer serves a period of "apprenticeship-like socialization" with an FTO. The new officer learns that the academy was just a rite of passage not to be taken seriously, that supervisors or managers are to be appeased, and that peers are the ones to whom the new officer owes allegiance and behavioral commitment by being willing to take risks backing up fellow officers and covering up for them in conflicts with management. As described by Van Maanen (1978), the traditional socialization or values transmission in policing resulted in officers being pitted against supervisors and managers.

If management values are to be transmitted to the new police employee and successfully controlled later, the police recruit must be exposed to the directing style of leadership. For successful values transmission, direction should be given in the training academy, by the field training officer, and by the immediate supervisor. The training academy experience must be more than lecturing and listening; it must involve frank discussion with case studies and simulations of the realities of making field decisions, using the organization's values as a basis for decisions. It should resemble an internship more than an introductory course in anatomy (Bayley & Bittner, 1989). For field training to be successful, the recommendations of McCampbell (1989) should be followed. The immediate supervisor should be more involved in managing by being out in the field with the street cop in the same vein as "managing by walking around" (Peters & Waterman, 1984).

WHAT DO WE NEED TO KNOW?

Further research is needed to understand the meaning and method of leadership and management in policing and to determine what works, how, and why. We need field research on management cops and on their interaction with other supervisory and operational levels. Van Maanen has given us some insight into two types of police sergeants. Yet our current notion of management cops is primarily based on Reuss-Ianni's observations of New York Police Department street cops. Are the perceptions of these street cops valid? Are they true for other bureaucratic police organizations? Are they valid in more participatory police organizations? Such questions need to be asked and answered.

Van Maanen's research on police socialization should be replicated because FTO programs have changed significantly since his field research (see McCampbell, 1989). Police organizations have sought to control the type of FTO used and what the new officer learns from the FTO. The role of supervisors in police socialization is a critical issue and should also be examined in this field research.

Southerland (1989, 1990) has begun the process of evaluating leadership techniques to define and identify *effective* leadership for policing. Further survey and field research directed specifically at the issue of leadership and management techniques and their relative effectiveness in terms of employee satisfaction and organizational goal achievement is needed. Through case studies of management and leadership the private sector has learned what works. Police managers and leaders need such studies to serve as prescriptive models for leadership development and training. Steinman (1986) cogently argues the importance of field research for evaluating police management and officer behavior.

There is a general belief that police leadership styles are more participatory now than in the early 1970s, but we need more broad-based research using a variety of methodological tools and conducted throughout a wide range of police agencies, not simply generalized from management studies conducted in a business setting, to understand the current style and status of police leadership and management.

REFERENCES

Auten, J.H. (1985). "Police Management in Illinois—1983." *Journal of Police Science and Administration,* 13,4:325-337.

Bayley, D.H. & E. Bittner (1989). "Learning the Skills of Policing." In R.G. Dunham & G.P. Alpert (eds.) *Critical Issues in Policing: Contemporary Readings*, pp. 87-110. Prospect Heights, IL: Waveland Press.

Bittner, E. (1983). "Introduction." In M. Punch (ed.) *Control in Police Organizations,* pp. 11-26. Cambridge, MA: MIT Press.

Blake, R. & J. Mouton (1964). *The Managerial Grid.* Houston, TX: Gulf Publishing Co.

Blanchard, K., P. Zigarmi & D. Zigarmi (1985). *Leadership and the One Minute Manager.* New York: William Morrow and Company.

Currie, C. (1988a). "First-Line Supervision: The Role of the Sergeant—Part One." *The Police Journal,* 61,4:312-329.

———— (1988b). "First-Line Supervision: The Role of the Sergeant—Part Two." *The Police Journal,* 62,1:69-84.

Dunning, C.M. & E. Hochstedler (1982). "Satisfaction with Communication in a Police Organization: 'Shooting the Shit,' 'Horsenecking,' and 'Brownie' Reports." In J.R. Greene (ed.) *Managing Police Work: Issues and Analysis,* pp. 140-157. Beverly Hills, CA: Sage Publications.

Hersey, P. & K. Blanchard (1969). *Management of Organizational Behavior: Utilizing Human Resources.* Englewood Cliffs, NJ: Prentice-Hall.

———— (1988). *Management of Organizational Behavior: Utilizing Human Resources,* 5th ed. Englewood Cliffs, NJ: Prentice-Hall.

Hoover, L.T. & E.T. Mader (1990). "Attitudes of Police Chiefs Toward Private Sector Management Principles." *American Journal of Police,* 9,4:25.

House, R.J. & T.R. Mitchell (1974). "Path-Goal Theory of Leadership." *Journal of Contemporary Business,* (Autumn):81-97.

Jermier, J.M. & L.J. Berkes (1979). "Leader Behavior in a Police Command Bureaucracy: A Closer Look at the Quasi-Military Model." *Administrative Science Quarterly,* 24,1:1-23.

Kuykendall, J.L. (1985). "Police Managerial Styles: A Grid Analysis." *American Journal of Police,* 4,1:38-70.

_____ & P.C. Unsinger (1982). "The Leadership Styles of Police Managers." *Journal of Criminal Justice,* 10:311-321.

Likert, R. (1961). *New Patterns of Management.* New York: McGraw-Hill.

_____ (1967). *The Human Organization.* New York: McGraw-Hill.

McCampbell, M.S. (1989). "Field Training for Police Officers: State of the Art," in R.G. Dunham & G.P. Alpert (eds.) *Critical Issues in Policing: Contemporary Readings,* pp. 111-120. Prospect Heights, IL: Waveland Press.

Ouchi, W.G. (1981). *Theory Z.* New York: Avon Books.

Peters, T. (1987). *Thriving on Chaos: Handbook for a Management Revolution.* New York: Harper and Row.

_____ & N. Austin (1985). *A Passion for Excellence: The Leadership Difference.* New York: Random House.

_____ & R.H. Waterman, Jr. (1982). *In Search of Excellence: Lessons from America's Best-Run Companies.* New York: Warner Books.

Reuss-Ianni, E. (1983). *Street Cops and Management Cops.* New Brunswick, NJ: Transaction Books.

Roberg, R.R. & J.J. Krichhoff (1985). "Applying Strategic Management Methods to Law Enforcement: Two Case Studies." *American Journal of Police,* 4,2:133-153.

Rokeach, M. (1973). *The Nature of Human Values.* New York: Macmillan.

Shanahan, G.W., J.D. Hunger & T.L. Wheelen (1979). "Organizational Profile of Police Agencies in the United States." *Journal of Police Science and Administration,* 7,3:354-360.

Southerland, M.D. (1989). "First-Line Police Supervision: Assessing Leadership Styles." Paper presented to the Southern Criminal Justice Association, Jacksonville, FL, October.

_____ (1990). "Police Patrol Supervision: Organizational Performance and Officer Satisfaction." Paper presented to the Academy of Criminal Justice Sciences, Denver, March.

Swanson, C.R. & L. Territo (1982). "Police Leadership and Interpersonal Communication Styles." In J.R. Greene (ed.) *Managing Police Work: Issues and Analysis,* pp. 123-139. Beverly Hills, CA: Sage Publications.

Steinman, M. (1986). "Managing and Evaluating Police Behavior." *Journal of Police Science and Administration,* 14,4:285-292.

Uchida, C.D. (1989). "The Development of American Police: An Historical Overview." In R.G. Dunham & G.P. Alpert (eds.) *Critical Issues in Policing: Contemporary Readings,* pp. 14-30. Prospect Heights, IL: Waveland Press.

Van Maanen, J. (1978). "Observations on the Making of Policemen." In P.K. Manning & J. Van Maanen (eds.) *Policing: A View From the Street,* pp. 292-308. Santa Monica, CA: Goodyear Publishing Company.

———— (1989). "Making Rank: Becoming an American Police Sergeant." In R.G. Dunham & G.P. Alpert (eds.) *Critical Issues in Policing: Contemporary Readings,* pp. 146-151. Prospect Heights, IL: Waveland Press.

Wasserman, R. & M.H. Moore (1988). "Values in Policing." *Perspectives on Policing.* Washington, DC: National Institute of Justice.

Weisburd, D., J. McElroy & P. Hardyman (1988). "Challenges to Supervision in Community Policing: Observations on a Pilot Project." *American Journal of Police,* 7,2:29-50.

Wilson, J.Q. (1978). *The Investigators: Managing FBI and Narcotics Agents.* New York: Basic Books.

Witte, J.H., L.F. Travis & R.H. Langworthy (1990). "Participatory Management in Law Enforcement." *American Journal of Police,* 9,4:1.

Subject Index

Author Index

About the Authors

Gary W. Cordner received his Ph.D. from Michigan State University and is on the faculty of the Department of Police Studies at Eastern Kentucky University. He has co-authored two books, *Planning in Criminal Justice Organizations and Systems* with John K. Hudzik (Macmillan, 1983) and *Introduction to Police Administration* with Robert Sheehan (Anderson, 1989), and written several articles and book chapters. Cordner has previously served as a police officer in Ocean City, Maryland and as police chief in St. Michaels, Maryland. He has been editor of the American Journal of Police since 1987.

John E. Eck is the Associate Director for Research for the Police Executive Research Forum (PERF). He has written extensively on criminal investigations management, problem-oriented policing, and police drug-control strategies. He has served as a consultant to the London Metropolitan Police on investigations management and has taught courses on research methods at the Canadian Police College. Eck has a Master of Public Policy degree from the Institute of Public Policy Studies at the University of Michigan and a Bachelor of General Studies from the same university. He is currently a doctoral student at the Institute of Criminal Justice and Criminology at the University of Maryland, College Park.

Larry K. Gaines is Professor and Chair of the Department of Police Studies at Eastern Kentucky University. He earned his M.S. at Eastern Kentucky University in 1972 and his Ph.D. at Sam Houston State University in 1975. Gaines began his police career as a communications officer with the Kentucky State Police and later became a police officer with the Lexington, Kentucky Police Department. His academic emphasis has been the study of organizations and management, including personnel administration and planning. He is the current Executive Director of the Kentucky Association of Chiefs of Police, a past president of the Academy of Criminal Justice Sciences, and co-author of *Police Administration: Design, Organization, Management, and Control Processes* (McGraw-Hill, 1991).

Donna C. Hale received her Ph.D. from Michigan State University's School of Criminal Justice. She is an Associate Professor of Criminal Justice at Shippensburg University. Her current research focuses on police recruit training and on the print media's portrayal of police activities. Presently, she is the coordinator of the law/judicial section of the Shippensburg University Model for Drug and Alcohol Prevention funded by the U.S. Department of Education.

Keith N. Haley is the Executive Director of the Ohio Peace Officer Training Council, the state's POST agency which oversees law enforcement and private security training at more than 200 locations, including 16 colleges and universities. He holds a B.S. from Wright State University and a M.S. in Criminal Justice from Michigan State University. Haley is a former faculty member and chair of the Criminal Justice Program at the University of Cincinnati. He has also worked in elementary education as an administrator and served as a police officer in Dayton, Ohio. His papers and publications have been primarily in the areas of education, training, and personnel management.

David W. Hayeslip, Jr., is presently a Visiting Senior Research Associate with the Office of Crime Prevention and Criminal Justice Research at the National Institute of Justice, U.S. Department of Justice. He is also an Associate Professor with the Department of Criminal Justice at the University of Baltimore. He received his bachelor's degree from the Pennsylvania State University and his master's degree and Ph.D. in Criminal Justice from Michigan State University. His research interests include police drug enforcement, illegal drug distribution in public housing, community policing, and homicide of police officers.

Knowlton W. Johnson is Director of the Urban Research Institute in the College of Urban and Public Affairs at the University of Louisville. He received his Ph.D. from Michigan State University in 1971. Johnson has published extensively with papers focusing on criminal victimization appearing in the *Journal of Urban Affairs, Victimology*, book chapters, and technical reports. Currently, he is completing a series of manuscripts based on a NIMH-funded panel study centering on criminal victimization and its psychological and behavioral consequences.

Victor E. Kappeler is an Assistant Professor in the Department of Criminal Justice, Central Missouri State University. He received his master's degree from Eastern Kentucky University and his Ph.D. from Sam Houston State University. Kappeler's research and publication activities have been in the areas of police liability and deviance. He has served as a liability consultant to numerous police departments and law firms, and is founder and editor of the *Police Liability Review.*

Robert H. Langworthy is Associate Professor of Criminal Justice at the University of Cincinnati. He is author of *The Structure of Police Organizations* and co-editor (with Belinda McCarthy) of *Older Offenders: Perspectives in Criminology and Criminal Justice.* His research interests include police organizational structure, evaluation of police practices, and public attitudes toward the police. Langworthy was elected as the first chair of the Police Section of the Academy of Criminal Justice Sciences.

Stephen L. Merker is Assistant Professor of Urban Policy at the University of Louisville. His expertise is in survey research, attitude measurement, questionnaire design, and systems science. His research related to criminal justice includes police attitudes, police perceptions of judges, police priorities, and job satisfaction of prison guards. He received his B.S. (physics), M.B.A., and Ph.D. (systems science) from the University of Louisville.

Elizabeth Reuss-Ianni is Director of Research at the Institute for Social Research in New York City. Prior to joining ISR she was Director of the Organized Crime Program at the National Council on Crime and Delinquency. She is the author of *Street Cops vs. Management Cops: The Two Cultures of Policing* (Transaction Books, 1982) and a number of articles in criminal justice and anthropological journals. She is also co-author with Francis A.J. Ianni of *A Family Business: Kinship and Social Control in an Organized Crime Family* (Russell Sage Foundation, 1972), and *The Crime Society: Organized Crime and Corruption in America* (New American Library, 1976).

Mittie D. Southerland is Associate Professor of Police Studies at Eastern Kentucky University, where she served previously as coordinator of the university's Fort Knox programs. She earned her M.S. at Eastern Kentucky University in 1973 and her Ph.D. at the University of Kentucky in 1984. A former criminal justice planner and juvenile counselor, her expertise is in the areas of administration, management, and supervision with particular emphasis on organizational environments and change in the police setting. Southerland is co-author of *Police Administration: Design, Organization, Management, and Control Processes* (McGraw-Hill, 1991) and has also published in the areas of juvenile justice and criminal justice education.

Elizabeth A. Stanko, Senior Lecturer in the Department of Law, Brunel University, United Kingdom, convenes the M.A. program in criminal justice. She has been active in the debates around violence against women since the late 1970s. Her publications include three edited volumes (featuring the most recent, *Women, Policing and Male Violence,* Routledge, 1989) and two single-authored books, *Intimate Intrusions* (Unwin Hyman, 1985) and *Everyday Violence* (Pandora, 1990). She is currently exploring how crime prevention advice and policy can better address people's experiences of personal violence, particularly in England and Wales.

Robert C. Trojanowicz is Director of the School of Criminal Justice at Michigan State University and Research Fellow in the Program in Criminal Justice Policy and Management, Kennedy School of Government, Harvard University. He has been Director of the National Center for Community Policing since its inception in 1982. He holds a B.S. in Police Administration, an M.S.W., and a Ph.D. in Social Science, all from Michigan State University. Trojanowicz has had experience with various police and social agencies. He is the author of several textbooks and has contributed numerous articles to management and criminal justice journals. Trojanowicz recently authored, with Bonnie Bucqueroux, *Community Policing: A Contemporary Perspective* (Anderson, 1990).

Deborah Lamm Weisel is a Research Associate with the Police Executive Research Forum (PERF) in Washington, D.C. Weisel is Associate Project Director for the Problem-Oriented Approach to Drug Enforcement project, a demonstration project applying the principles of problem-oriented policing to drug problems in five cities. Weisel is involved in conducting an innovative case study documentation of decision-making in municipal law enforcement agencies. She has also done extensive work in issues related to drugs and public housing and is author of *Tackling Drugs in Public Housing: A Guide for Police.* Prior to joining PERF, Weisel was a government reporter for a major North Carolina daily newspaper. She has extensive experience in the field of communications and intergovernmental relations. Weisel holds a bachelor's degree from the University of North Carolina at Chapel Hill and a Master's of Public Affairs from North Carolina State University.